Set A Seal Upon My Heart

A Devotional Study of The Song of Solomon

Sarah A. Neisen

Editors: Krista Wagner & Kelly Casbourne

Cover Image: BetiBup Design

Interior Design: Dxeralam

First printing 2020

ISBN: 978-1-7353974-1-2 (ebook)

ISBN: 978-1-7353974-0-5 (paperback)

Praise for

Set A Seal Upon My Heart

Sarah Neisen's study of the Song of Solomon is insightful, delightful, and motivating. I love the way she points us to God's love and her special skill of finding meaningful definitions for Hebrew words, which makes her text come alive.

– Kathy Collard Miller, speaker, author of over 55 books including God's Intriguing Questions: 40 Old Testament Devotions Revealing God's Nature

I thoroughly enjoyed how Sarah was able to bring the New Testament reality of one's relationship with the Lord into the Song of Solomon. Sarah has a vast knowledge of the scriptures, and this is a devotional study that will challenge and inspire mature believers into a deeper walk with Jesus Christ.

–Doyle VanGelder MDiv Bethel College

Acknowledgements

Father in Heaven, thank You for loving me and sending Your son.

Jesus my Savior, Bridegroom, and Friend, all I have is yours.

My husband Lee, you are daily proof of God's love and grace.

My son Joshua, your love of the Lord motivates and encourages me every day.

To the many ministers and teachers of the Word who have motivated, encouraged, and equipped me, this book is a testament to your teaching I can do all things through Christ.

Table of Contents

"The world was never as worthy as on the day that the Song of Songs was given to Israel, for all the Writings are holy, whereas the Song of Songs is the holiest of the holy."

-Rabbi Rashi

This is the Song of Songs, excellent above any others, for it is wholly taken up with describing the excellences of Christ, and the love between him and his redeemed people.

-Matthew Henry

Introduction

An Inspired Author

The Song of Songs, the most excellent of them all, which is Solomon's.

The Song of Solomon 1:1

King Solomon penned over one thousand psalms during his reign over Israel, and our first insight into those psalms is this song, is the most excellent of them all. All the psalms of David and Solomon show the faithfulness of the Father, but they are written from a human perspective in response to discontent and circumstance. In the days of Solomon, this was true for the covenant people, as the redemption for sin had not yet been given. Now as believers in Christ our righteousness is forever.

It is amazing this insight, into the deep intimacy of Christ and His church, came through Solomon. Considered by many the wisest of men, Solomon still revealed his sinful human nature in the slow distancing of himself from the Father as he aged. This study is not of Solomon himself, but it is important to understand his beginning, his life as king, and his end.

In the beginning of Solomon's reign, the influence of his Father, David, was strong. Upon taking the throne, Solomon makes a sacrifice and asks the Lord for wisdom. The author of 1 Kings notes in the third chapter the influence of Solomon's mother, Bathsheba, was also present in his life.

Bathsheba was the wife of Uriah the Hittite, whom David had killed when he took his wife in an adulterous affair. The Hittites were known to be pagan and made offerings in the high places. We read in 1 Kings Solomon allowed the high places of sacrifice to remain in Israel during his reign.

At some point during his rule, we note a downward turning, and we find the riches of Solomon mentioned before his wisdom in 1 Kings 10:23. Precious insight into this turning is given at the beginning of 1 Kings chapter 11 when we are told Solomon loved foreign women from the neighboring lands. In all, Solomon had 700 wives and 300 concubines.

This man who wrote this 'most excellent song' was the same man who wrote the book of Ecclesiastes, a book of regrets, a book of vanity and vain pleasures of life. This is exemplified in Ecclesiastes 7:28 where Solomon writes, "Which I am seeking but have not found, one upright man among a thousand have I found, but an upright woman among all those have I not found."

With the obvious contempt of his wives and concubines written in Ecclesiastes, one must wonder how people view the Song of Solomon as a letter between lovers. The love, or lack of love, of Solomon for his wives was evident, but with powerful passages such as, "I am my beloveds and my beloved is mine" and "You are altogether beautiful, my love; there is no flaw in you." We clearly see Solomon understood unfailing love.

I suggest then that this song is one of wisdom from a man who saw the pursuit of life's pleasures as meaningless and the pursuit of God and His love as supreme. In synagogues, the Song of Solomon is read every Passover, which suggests a strong connection to our Passover lamb.

As we progress through the song I hope and pray you experience this beautiful progression of love and intimacy with Christ our Bridegroom. With many allegorical references and subtle uses of specific words, this song is an intimate view of the process of

discipleship for new believers.

PART 1

Foundations of Love The Song of Solomon 1:2-3:4

CHAPTER 1

A Song of Love & Consecration

Awakening To Love

Let him kiss me with the kisses of his mouth! For your love is better than wine!

The Song of Solomon 1:2

This greatest of songs begins with a fervent declaration of love from the bride, and we are immediately affected by the song's play upon our hearts. The Father makes Himself known to us even when we face difficult circumstances. In awe of His mercy and greatness, our hearts settle, peace reigns, and all things are new. We learn of His abundant love and that we were never out of His sight or reach.

Abundant joy springs from this miracle of renewal in our hearts, causing us to cry out. Kisses we all yearn for are the touch every soul desires from the bridegroom. Intimacy is possible with Christ, yet in our newness, to life we don't understand the paths we must walk to acquire its fullness. This path we walk toward our bridegroom ends with our spirit and soul cleaving to Him. No one else can satisfy.

This word translated "kiss" not only indicates a touch of the lips but also a fastening upon something. In other verses in scripture, the word is translated as equipping. A kiss is a touch of the mouth, so why does she say with his mouth? The word used and translated mouth doesn't denote the literal mouth one would use to speak but it indicates all things proceed from it. She implies that not only does she desire a kiss or equipping, but she wishes all those things she is touched by and equipped with come from His mouth. Those things may be his breath, speech, and commands.

How awe-inspiring this breath of life is. Our bridegroom Jesus redeemed us and restored us to right standing with the Father so we can live spiritually, gaining what Adam lost in the Fall. Not only did Jesus restore us to the Father, but He also sent the Holy Spirit, the breath of Heaven, so we would be comforted and equipped by the Spirit to do every good work.

Genesis 2:7 "Then the Lord God formed man from the dust of the ground and breathed into his nostrils the breath of spirit of life, and man became a living being." AMP

As we see in this second verse the bride cries out for her desire be fulfilled immediately. However, we must understand to wholly belong to Him we cannot belong to ourselves. The marriage vows unite a bride and bridegroom to a covenant private in nature, yet visible in life.

Marriage requires one to leave the Father and mother of our birth and cleave to our spouse. We become one flesh and together something new in the eyes of God. Similarly, when we confess faith in Christ, we begin this cleaving process, and our salvation allows His touch and access to our lives. To embrace our role as the bride of Christ our old man must be mortified, and we must embrace the new creature in Him.

The Song of Solomon shows us this spiritual progress. To first grasp Jesus, we must come to know Him as our Savior. Unfortunately, this basic knowledge of Him is where many believers stop and fail to address the deeper things found in Him. Salvation is a union of betrothal to Christ, but it is not a marriage with the deep intimacies the bride desires (Rev3:22).

Never forget as we progress in our new life at all stages of our walk we are well able to produce fruit for the kingdom. Salvation does not make us fruitful but allows us to become fruitful for the kingdom. We seek Him daily growing in relationship with Him, and the fruits of the spirit are stirred and made alive in our spirit. Appreciating His faithfulness is the source of our fruitfulness.

Let's unpack this verse:

Let him touch, fasten upon, equip me with the kisses of his breath, speech, and commands. For your love is better than wine!

The love of Christ on the cross is better than any temple sacrifice, and the work of redemption not only provided a fallen world with salvation but a restoration to right standing with the Father. The wine offering given during the temple sacrifices of the first lamb was an offering for sin. An offering Jesus freely gave on the cross as our perfect and spotless lamb. The Lord's sacrifice is better than any temple offering that only covered sin and allowed sin consciousness to remain. By taking sin upon Himself, Jesus erased our sin and our guilty conscious (Heb. 12:22).

How mighty was the joy Jesus experienced to endure the cross for it! There was great joy fulfilling the words spoken by the prophets. He saw great joy in the church arrayed in glory, and His bride seated with Him at the marriage supper clothed in white. Every believer calling upon His name filled Him with joy. His love for us is never-ending.

This wine, while used daily in the temple sacrifices, was the natural fruit of the vine. Jesus said He is the vine, and we are the branches (John 15:5). The fruit of His faithfulness and nourishment in our lives produces spiritual fruit and new wine far better than wine one might drink on earth. No longer are sacrifices poured out over altars of stone. They now pour out within the hearts of believers.

The maiden in this song is pursuing her bridegroom alone. Why do you think this pursuit of Jesus must be done individually?

Read Romans 5:17

Have there been times you've felt condemned by your sin after salvation? What does this verse imply about that condemnation and guilt?

Read John 16:7

Why did Jesus need to leave the disciples? If He loved the believers and left so the Holy Spirit could come what does this imply about the gift He sent?

Prayer: Thank You Lord for the joy and peace of a renewed heart. I pray that you would equip me to do Your will and give me strength through the Holy Spirit to accomplish all those tasks. Reveal to me how You see me, and help me understand the joy You saw before the cross in Jesus' name. Amen.

Activation: The most amazing gift believers experience is the salvation of our souls. It's humbling to share the love of God with others. If you're like most people, someone invited you to church or maybe witnessed to you at work. Know this: God wishes to use you in the same way. Are you ready? The most effective way to reach people with the love of God is simply sharing our story. It's called giving a testimony. In your journal, write down the story of how Jesus reached you with His love. While we don't read our story to someone, simply writing it down will solidify all that you would share with someone when God calls you to witness. When you're done, pray and ask God to bring someone into your life to share your story with. You'll be amazed at how many people are touched!

A Sacrifice of Love

The odor of your ointments is fragrant; your name is like perfume poured out. Therefore, do the maidens love you.

The Song of Solomon 1:3

Time and again throughout the Old Testament, God answers the sweet savor of sacrifices offered in His name. The first was the sacrifice of Noah in Genesis 8:21. Once the Lord breathed in the savor of the sacrifice offered, He vowed to never again destroy the whole earth. As believers in Christ, we too carry the savor of Jesus.

The graces of God poured out to us carry a soothing fragrance of healing and deliverance. When God pours He does so in considerable measure. It is not halting, or a simple stroke of balm on a surface wound, but an ongoing flow of grace, mercy, and communion with the Holy Spirit which heals our innermost pains. The name of Jesus is precious healing ointment poured out for us. Through His name we find victory over every situation and circumstance in our lives.

Christ's heart is grieved by the young maidens who love Him because of what they gain from Him. They are so young in their understanding of His true and pure love, they only draw on what they may receive from Him. Human nature many times blinds us to all except for the pleasure we experience loving. We should rather experience love itself, and the One from whom it flows.

In our minds many times we view love as a reflection of our inner desires. Our feelings toward people and things drive us to call them our own. The pure love of Jesus will grow us in ways we don't yet understand, but it will be growth away from selfish desires and feelings of ownership, to pure communion of heart and joyful abiding.

Do you have any strained relationships or past hurts from people? Have you forgiven them? Have you asked God to heal your hurt and pain?

Read 2 Corinthians 2:15-16

Reading these verses and thinking of sacrifice, what do you believe the 'sweet fragrances' are in your life? Can you have many fragrances? How so?

Read Isaiah 53:12

What do you believe the 'spoils' are that Christ receives? Read also Luke 22:37

Prayer: Lord, I pray that you would search my heart today. Thank You for revealing to me any person I need to forgive and for the fragrant oil of Your name that will soothe the hurt they caused. Help me see You for more than what I might gain and help me to understand the depth of your love in Jesus' name. Amen.

Activation: Forgiveness isn't for the person we forgive. It's for us. In prayer you asked God for someone you needed to forgive. Ask Him now how you should forgive and do so. Is He saying to call them? Maybe write a letter for them to read? Whatever it is, shake off the shackles of unforgiveness today and move forward in all that God has for you.

Our Hearts Cry

Draw me! We will run after you! The king brings me into his apartments. We will be glad and rejoice in you. We will recall (when we are favored) with your love, more fragrant than wine. The upright (are not offended at your choice, but sincerely) love you.

The Song of Solomon 1:4

Finding ourselves sated by the simple love of receiving, we perceive there are more than superficial experiences available. It is why all hearts cry out 'Draw me near!' This word מָשַׁךְ *mashak* translated "draw me" is many times translated as develop or plant. The heart of the betrothed is crying out here to develop something within her so she may run after Him with abandon. When God answers and draws us to Himself, we should race after what He shows. Where He leads me I should follow for He only has good things for me.

Once we give ourselves over to 'running after thee', the difficulty of our race no longer matters. Instead, we choose to fix our sights on the One who draws us to Him rather than the difficulty of the path He leads us down. Here we perceive the development God initiates in us, and the Holy Spirit begins to dig deeper, bringing us closer to the person of God.

The apartments of the king are where he abides. This bedchamber is the innermost private place where we as believers may enter. To find rest in these chambers, we must understand the gifts, grace, and goodness of God are always flowing from Him. They are a product of who He is, but they are not Him. We must focus our eyes on Him, setting aside all selfish desires to comprehend all He is.

The betrothed begins to understand it's only by the love and gift of Jesus that this journey towards union is possible. This love is deeper and more fulfilling than any bitterness of law and carnal sacrifice. Those fleshly things harden hearts and dull the senses to the Word and Truth. Those who are upright by His sacrifice do not balk at the desire for intimacy with any person of the Trinity; indeed, they find in their innermost being they desire and need it as well.

What first drew you to Jesus? How did this drawing affect situations in your life at the time?

Read Jeremiah 31:3

How does the Lord draw us to Him?

Read 2 Corinthians 8:9

How do you recognize the grace of Jesus in your life? Do you feel there are ways you could recognize His grace more often?

Read Hebrews 10:22

How do we draw near to God? What is an 'evil conscience'? Why do we need to be free from one?

Prayer: Lord, stir my heart to run after You with abandon. Bring me closer to Your heart so that I would know You more, and help me keep my eyes focused on You. Thank You for developing in me a hunger for only those things that give You glory in Jesus' name. Amen.

Activation: Is there something hindering you? Maybe you've messed up and you're worried God is angry. Whatever holds you back from running after Him needs to be loosed. Take a sheet of paper and write down all the things you feel 'sin conscience' about. Lies, addictions, anger, bitterness, whatever they are write them out, and when you're done burn the paper or tear it up. As you tear up the paper or burn it thank Jesus that all things hindering you can't stand His name and flee. Praise Him for deliverance! If you feel your sin is a recurring problem, find another believer to pray with you and hold you accountable for righteousness. Everyone needs accountability in this process of growth.

We Need You

I am so black; but [you are] lovely and pleasant. O you daughters of Jerusalem, [I am as dark] as the tents of [the Bedouin tribe] Kedar, like the [beautiful] curtains of Solomon!

The Song of Solomon 1:5

Once she leaves the presence of the king's divine bedchamber, this betrothed finds she is black. Beautiful and pleasant, yet black as though stained. Weakness and inability to survive and thrive in this world tainted by sin becomes readily apparent when we seek after Him. The black stain of sin and the heavy curtain in place separating us from the Father is now all we can consider.

Faced with feelings of separation from God by our sin or feelings of unworthiness, we must remember Jesus poured Himself out for us. The perception of our eyes can mislead us. We have been washed, but we often find ourselves clinging to our flesh. This blackness can also be found in our minds. Until our salvation through Christ, we thought as the world, did as the world, and felt as the world.

How often do we compare our spiritual state to another? This beautiful bride-to-be finds herself comparing her stains to the perceived beauty of another. These daughters of Jerusalem appear beautiful, but we must never fall into the trap of comparison within the kingdom, for no one but the Lord knows the hearts of men. The sin of comparison is one of envy. In the Old Testament Sarah envied Hagar's ability to provide and heir to Abraham.

The tents of Kedar were black upon the land. Kedar, one of twelve grandsons through Ishmael, would found a tribe of people who covered the Arabian Peninsula. Eventually, this tribe of people was cursed to suffer at the hands of Nebuchadnezzar. The word Kedar means darkness or all things that stem from the darkness.

It was not only a tribe of people dwelling in the harshest of lands, but a visual representation of man's attempt in helping God. Though Abraham was told he would Father a nation through whom the promise would come, he found in his human nature God's timing was not pleasing to his flesh.

Deep within our human nature detests the idea of waiting. Christianity itself is a lesson in waiting on the Lord. Abraham needed to wait for the promise of God through Sarah. By believing he knew better than God how this miracle of a son should come, he created schism within his household. Through Hagar he had a son, and to this day the descendants of Ishmael and Isaac fight over the land of promise.

Patience and humility are not only fruits of the spirit but are the spiritual answers to pride in our lives. Pride caused this bride to consider her own faults and failures, but patience and humility will lead her to developing a deeper relationship with the bridegroom.

The curtains of Solomon spanned 60 by 30 feet and were nearly 4 inches thick. They cloaked the Holy of Holies and the Ark of the Covenant from the view of worshipers in the temple enclosure. The curtains shielded the sinful people from the Spirit of God hovering over the ark. Once a year the high priest stood before the ark to make sacrifice for the people, but Jesus cried out on the cross 'It is finished' and the atoning sacrifice was made once and for all. At His cry the curtains of Solomon tore top to bottom and the presence of God was made accessible to all. How wonderful the curtains were torn from above so all could come!

What did the King's chamber reveal to the bride?

Have you compared your walk with God to another's? Why?

Was there a time when you did something to 'help' God along? What was the result?

Do you have thoughts, feelings, or actions similar to before you were saved?

Read Philippians 3:8-9

How did Paul deal with his blackness?

Read Hebrews 6:19-20

What did Jesus do for all who believe? What happens as a result?

Read Isaiah 1:18; Romans 3:23

Prayer: Lord, teach me patience and humility as I walk this path of sanctification. Let me be attentive to the Holy Spirit and walk the way of righteousness. When I do stumble Lord, let me be swift to confess and swift to believe You still love me. Help me stop comparing myself to others, and let my life be a place where You are glorified in Jesus' name. Amen.

Activation: After prayer, ask the Father how He sees you. Write all the words that come to your mind in your journal. It's all right if there are only a few or if you fill the whole page. This is an exercise to help you hear from the Father on a regular basis. We often overlook His speaking because we don't expect it, or in some cases we don't believe the words we hear. How many of these words were positive? Did you write any negative words? Where do you think negative words come from? Read 1 Corinthians 13.

Lord, Help My Mess

[Please] do not look at me, [she said, for] I am swarthy. [I have worked out] in the sun and it has left its mark upon me. My mother's sons were angry with me, and they made me keeper of the vineyards; but my own vineyard [my complexion] I have not kept.

The Song of Solomon 1:6

Purification of our hearts as our old self dies leads us to view ourselves with new eyes. We often believe our sin should cause God to overlook us. Instead, we need His gaze to solidify our salvation by the Son of His love. Adam and Eve covered themselves to hide their imperfections and insecurities from the Father, but we must show our need for His grace and mercy by showing that our outer beauty is only skin deep.

Keeping the vineyards may appear laborious, but the Lord uses this as an example of this poor bride's true state. כֶּרֶם *kerem* the word translated "vineyard" can mean an actual vineyard, but it can also mean a place from which ideas and culture get their roots. The bride is not saying she was slaving in the sun; rather, we find her toiling in the fields of man's ideas exposed in a personal way in this 'vineyard' of a fallen culture.

Toiling under the curse of man's ideas God instructs her to instead cultivate righteous fruit from the one who is the true vine in the vineyard she hadn't kept. The bride-to-be is painfully aware her Father in Heaven is not the same as her family on earth. The ties she shares with them and this world subjects her to work and exposure.

Trees are covered and arrayed in beauty during the spring and summer, and ornaments in our lives may insinuate joy and beauty to those on the outside. However, during our journey toward marriage to the bridegroom we must allow old thoughts and ideas to pass away and all things to become new. The bride no longer suffers the curse of blackness in her mind and its effects because her bridegroom delivered her.

Winter season is a time of growth and nourishment for all believers. Plants appear barren, but beneath our feet they push out new roots and strengthen ones already present. As we push new roots into the truth of the Word, we grow away from the world and its ideas. Winter is

13

also a time of pruning in vineyards, and we all must prune away wrong desire. By pruning off those things not the will of God for us, we cause new growth and vigor for the things of the kingdom.

However bleak things may look on the surface, this is a time of establishment and growth. Only by exposing our flaws to the Father are we healed and restored. We are told by the Lord that His gaze, his consideration, and discernment would cause the sinful people to perish, but now through Jesus, we are told to come boldly before the throne of grace.

What works in the field of men are you doing? Have you asked God what to do in the field He has called you to?

Read Colossians 3:1-3

How would you define 'your vineyard' in light of this verse?

Read Galatians 2:20-21

What is your definition of 'He lives in me' and how would you apply this to your life today?

Prayer: Lord, I thank You that You help me renew my mind. Prune away all wrong desires in my thoughts and in my heart, and help me cultivate thinking and acting in line with Your word. Show me where to change and lead me along the paths of righteousness in Jesus' name. Amen.

Activation: Ask the Lord to reveal to you things you are still working on and striving for in the world. Write them in your journal. Over the next few days ask the Lord to show you where you can cultivate godly desires in place of those things. Write them in your journal as a goal to begin cultivating His desires this month.

Longing For You

Tell me, O you whom my soul loves, where you pasture your flock, where you make it lie down at noon. For why should I [as I think of you] be as a veiled one straying beside the flocks of your companions?

The Song of Solomon 1:7

The purest desire of any heart who has called on Jesus as their Savior is to know Him as Shepherd. His gentle nature as leader and guider of those who follow begets a desire to know His paths and ways. It is He whom our soul loves and desires, and all people desire the satisfaction that only comes from the One who is the Bread of Life. Understanding He is our sole Supplier causes us to hunger and thirst no more.

As a benevolent Shepherd, Jesus offers us perfect rest and peace whenever we are under the heat of tests and trials. When under persecution from the enemy, we call on Him and find comfort under His wings. We must avoid the desire to turn aside and follow the other flocks that go astray from the true Shepherd. How often does it happen that believers shout for joy, then as the tests and trials of faith come, turn aside from following a simpler path or one they should never travel upon?

The wanderings of many mark a failure to seek His guidance and council in their lives. The Word tells us to follow the example of Jesus, and daily He prayed and sought the will of the Father. She asks her bridegroom why she would want to wander like those blinded to the truth of the Good Shepherd. He is the one who will lead her to rest in true comfort. To stray from the One who will lead her and guide her in all truth would lead to her own eyes being veiled.

Read 2 Corinthians 3:16

What is the significance of an unveiled face?

Read John 6:32-35

How does one partake of this bread? This bread is compared to the manna given in the wilderness. What is the significance of this?

Read 1 Corinthians 1:12-13

Who are we to follow? Have you found yourself following others?

Read Proverbs 4:18

Describe the pathway of the just. If this is the path to spiritual maturity, whom are we following?

Prayer: Thank You Lord that I hear Your voice. I pray that You give me ears to hear even clearer the way in which I am to go. Lead me on the path of righteousness and help me keep focused on You. Lord, speak to me when I'm turning aside or listening to others so that I may only follow you in Jesus' name. Amen.

Activation: Ask the Lord what His path for you is over the next month. Write down what you hear in your journal and set a goal to follow this for that time. Activation is all about learning to hear His voice clearly in every situation.

Distractions to Overcome

If you do not know [where your lover is], O you fairest among women, run along, follow the tracks of the flock, and [amuse yourself by] pasturing your kids beside the shepherds' tents.

The Song of Solomon 1:8

The world's thoughts concerning an honest heart question will never point to our Lord and Savior. These poor souls seek and find the obvious answer. Yes, He may be found with His followers, but we are on a journey to know Him intimately. While the word teaches all fit jointly within the larger body of Christ, the church, The Holy Spirit himself indwells us, and He reveals Christ.

Do we search out our bridegroom in the presence of His followers, in the words of His under-shepherds (pastors of the local church), or do we instead look inward to the abiding presence of our King of Kings and Lord of Lords? Had this betrothed instead relied on this personal relationship with Jesus, she could not only ask questions of Him but expect answers to be given.

The bride asks where she may find the one whom her soul is seeking. When we approach Jesus in this way, as one who desires Him, answers will be given; however, the answer here is a strange one. If you do not know (some translations say "comprehend") run along, and follow the tracks of all the others who traveled before you, follow along the navigating through the world, and amuse yourself by following the tracks and worn down paths left by others.

A similar question was asked of Jesus in Luke 2:48. His mother and Joseph were returning from Jerusalem, and after days of walking they realized Jesus wasn't with them. When they finally found Him in the temple teaching, Mary asked why He was there. His answer was simple. I must be about My Father's business. You would never find Jesus perusing His own agenda, nor would you find Him outside the Father's will.

The life of Jesus was one of total surrender to the Father's will. We must be aware man can't offer anything of eternal value, and only God gives us true rest and nourishment. Seek out the pasture where He dwells and nourishes the flock. Busy minds often make it difficult for new believers to acknowledge the indwelling presence of God. His voice is drowned out by our list of tasks and necessary duties.

New believers in Christ will learn a great deal of discernment when in fellowship with mature believers. The guidance of His under-shepherds and other elders should always lead us to a more intimate relationship with our bridegroom. It's vital we keep focused on our Lord and seek Him in the Word rather than in the words of pastors or elders. Many ask and don't seek. They run along in their own way, pursing their own lusts, but we must always remember the Word promises if we seek we shall find.

Have you sought God and been disappointed? Where and how did you seek Him?

Read Matthew 7:7

What does this verse say about persistence in seeking the Lord? What door do you feel is opened?

Read 2 Corinthians 13:5

How do you test your faith? What faith tests have you passed recently? Have you failed any faith tests? How do you feel Matthew 7:7 can encourage you to try again?

Read Ephesians 4:11-13

Who are the under-shepherds we are to follow? Who might the kids be who follow the bride?

Prayer: Thank You Jesus for sending the Holy Spirit for all believers, and I praise You that He continually reveals You to me. I attune myself to the Holy Spirit's leading in my life and renew my mind to listen intently in Jesus' name. Amen.

Activation: It's easy as believers to attend church on Sunday and not read the Word the other six days of the week. Today I'd like you to sit down and ask God what you can do about making Bible Study a part of those six days. Can you read one chapter at the breakfast table? Is it possible to read a few verses over lunch? Can you listen to an audio Bible on your way to work? Don't feel you need to tackle huge amounts of scripture at a time. You can read through the Bible even if you only read ten minutes every day. Write your plan in your journal and share with us what God's plan is for your study on twitter.

@DiscipleshipTr1 on twitter. We love to partner with you and encourage you!

Let Them Go

O my love you remind me of my [favorite] mare in the chariot spans of Pharaoh.

The Song of Solomon 1:9

Praises of the king, whom our soul craves, are one of the many gentle touches we perceive as we find our course. The most prized possessions of Solomon's day were the horses of Pharaoh. Pure bred Arabians were symbols of strength while beauty adorned the chariots. They were the best trained and the most costly, but more importantly for the bridegroom they were mares of endurance. The courses set before them were arduous but everyone was well able to finish them.

However, this compliment is a gentle reminder that though the betrothed loves Him and is seeking after Him, she is still subject to the worldly kings. He does not compare her to something of his own, but rather a prized object of the Pharaoh. Throughout the Word, Egypt is used as a type of the world and all its idols. The bride exhibits many virtues that will carry her far, but she is still tied to the world's ways. Being tied to the world is a burden and many don't know they are still running the worlds races until they are shown by the King.

Can you think of ways you have been relying on the world? What can you do differently?

Read Isaiah 36:6

Why might Egypt be called a broken reed? What does it do to those who lean on or rely on it?

Read Job 39:19-25

How might believers be like the striving horse? What words are used to describe the horse?

Prayer: Holy Spirit, search the deepest parts of me. Show me where I'm still holding on to the world. Lord, repair my trust so that I'm not afraid to lean on You. Reveal to me even more of Your love and forgive my stubbornness. Help me to endure this race so I would finish well and hear from You on that day well done (Matt. 25:23).

Activation: We all hold on. Living in the world can make it hard to trust completely. Jesus is like no other. In your journal write down where you are holding on to the world. Ask the Holy Spirit why you're holding on and what you can do to let go. Are you afraid that a situation will happen again? Be honest with your bridegroom and listen intently to what He says.

Truth In Love

Your cheeks are comely with ornaments, your neck with strings of jewels.

The Song of Solomon 1:10

You've adorned yourself, he says. These strings of jewels around your neck are tied, He says, bound to you in the same manner in which a burden would be bound to your neck. This word צַוָּארָה tsavvâ'râh, translated neck means to bind with knots upon the back of the neck. It's the place oxen are yoked and animals are tied for pasture.

The bridegroom is again pointing to the chains fettering the betrothed to this world and its ruler. How else could we shed the cares and burdens of this world if Our Shepherd did not make us aware? While the jewels of the world may appear to be beautiful and valuable to us, it is our heavenly treasure He desires us to focus on.

These strings of jewels tie her to her master like a reign and a bridle. The yoke of this ruler is heavy, and whether it is cares of this life or our desires of the flesh, the whip of this world's master is harsh and unforgiving.

What burdens of the world do you feel you're carrying? How might you give those burdens to Jesus?

Read Revelation 3:18

What does this gold represent? The white clothes?

Prayer: Lord, I give my cares and burdens to You today. You say your yoke is easy and your burden is light. Every chain holding me back is broken now in Jesus name.

Activation: Many times in the Old Testament the Lord would have the children of Israel do something called a prophetic act. One example would be walking around Jericho 7 times and shouting. Their actions were in obedience and moved things in spiritual places. Today you'll do a prophetic act. Imagine those chains bound to your neck. Take a hold of them now and break them. Thank Jesus that He carries those cares and burdens. Whenever you think of those cares again, say out loud that He holds them now and they aren't yours to carry.

Put Off The Old

We will make for you chains and ornaments of gold, studded with silver.

The Song of Solomon 1:11

These gold chains are the adornments of the bridegroom purchased and refined by the refiner's fire. They are not laid upon the neck as a burden. Here he is saying 'I come with burdens as well, but they are beautiful and good for you.'

These golden chains and ornaments are the same words used to describe the chains and ornaments found within Solomon's temple. The chains themselves were drawn across the inner temple enclosure, while the floor, walls, and ceiling of the Holy of Holies was paneled with ornaments. The golden altar of incense and tables of show-bread were continual reminders of the need for the bread of life and the sacrifices for holiness.

Those things we are instructed to do by God are the gold, silver, and precious stones that stand the test before Jesus. We are all able to do 'good' things but not all good things are God things. Maybe you've been asked to help with a function at church, and rather than immediately say yes, pray and ask God what you should do. If you feel peace or a yes in your heart, say yes! If you feel like something's not quite right or you feel reluctant, it's okay to say no. It's possible God has something else for you to do that day.

Read Matthew 11:30

How might the yoke of Jesus be easy to bear while the yoke of Satan is heavy?

Read 1 Corinthians 3:11-13

In light of this verse what do you feel the jewels of the world around the bride's neck might represent? What do the gold and silver represent in this verse?

Prayer: Father, I thank You for making a way to enter the Holy of Holies. I pray You reveal to me the gold chains which are light to carry and adorn those who love You and do Your will. In Jesus' name. Amen.

Activation: If you're like me, requests to help come pretty regularly. When I was a new believer I felt like I needed to say yes to everything. It was for God after all, right? Not so. We are all part of the Body of Christ and have specific duties for the kingdom, and not everything you're asked to do is what God wants you to do. Think about the requests that have come your way recently and write them down in your journal. Over the next couple of days ask God about each one. Is this for you to do? Or should you say no? It's not easy to say no to good things, but watch what God brings your way when you learn to trust and rely on Him for answers in every area.

It Was Finished

While the king sits at his table, my spikenard [my absent lover] sends forth [his] fragrance [over me].

The Song of Solomon 1:12

Again the risen King presides over all at the table, but the fragrant anointing oil of his death is strong. By His death all who call upon Him are victorious. Revelation 3:20 tells us that those who answer the call of the Lord are those who will dine with Him, and that the king's table is richly appointed.

Jesus is our anointed High Priest and Advocate, but He was not anointed by the ruler of the Jews. Rather He was anointed by the humblest of people. The one Simon called 'a most notorious sinner'.

Luke 7:37 "Now there was a woman in the city who was [known as] a sinner; and when she found out that He was reclining *at the table* in the Pharisee's house, she brought an alabaster vial of perfume; and standing behind Him at His feet, weeping, she began wetting His feet with her tears, and wiped them with the hair of her head, and [respectfully] kissed His feet [as an act signifying both affection and submission] and anointed them with the perfume."

The Law of Moses appointed men to lead temple worship and service, but they were all men subject to sin. Our new covenant is led by a High Priest who knew no sin, and by His sacrifice brought us newness of life. By His death we were given all authority and made priests to serve our God. It was fitting then that Mary would anoint the High Priest of this new and better covenant as a representative of the church and its cross of forgiveness.

Revelation 5:10 "You have made them to be a kingdom [of royal subjects] and priests to our God; and they will reign on the earth."

Read 1 Kings 4:22
Describe the provision of the king's table.

Read Hebrews 5:13-15
Who is able to partake with the Lord at His table?

Read Jeremiah 15:16
What happens when one feasts on the Word?

Prayer: Thank You Lord that I have a place at the King's table. I pray you give me wisdom and discernment what I am to do with the cross of Christ. As I feast on the Truth of your Word, I pray that it would begin to take root in me, and that I will begin to produce fruits of righteousness in my life.

Activation: In the Old Testament, to anoint something was to set it apart for God's use. Jesus was set apart just as we are. Ask God what you have been set apart for and write His answer in your journal.

A Denial of Self

My beloved [shepherd] is to me like a [scent] bag of myrrh that lies in my bosom.

The Song of Solomon 1:13

However glorious His current place, we must recognize the sacrifice made so we might become the righteousness of God in Christ. This bundle of Myrrh with all its thorns is not a bridegroom we embrace without pain. Our Christ does not give us this bundle, but rather He is the bundle. It is because of her love for Him she suffers. The cross of Christ which bought our redemption came with a price, one given out of love and for joy. Spikenard and myrrh anointed the dead and here anoints the new temple of our hearts for the Holy Spirit.

Jesus tells us to daily take up our cross and follow after Him. We must say it is my bloodied bridegroom, crucified and poured out for me, which nourishes my soul. Death to our selfish ways is the cross we bear. We don't bear the burden of sin any longer for He took it upon Himself, but the separation of ourselves to the will of the Father will cause our flesh pain. We must lay aside those things we desire and seek first the kingdom, for one day we shall all stand before our bridegroom and give an account of this life.

Many believers fear the judgment seat because they believe it is an accounting for our sin, but this isn't true. It is an account of what was done in this life, and this judgment is a decision whether what was done in our lives was excellent or worthless. Was our motive to follow Jesus based on what He would give me? Is it to follow Him so we might know Him and lead others to Him? It is a shift in our perspective from earthly concerns to eternal kingdom concerns. What do we do with this cross of Christ?

In what ways do you deny yourself to follow the Lord? How often do you think about eternity with Jesus?

Read Mark 16:15

What are we called to do by Jesus?

Read Galatians 2:20

How do we obey this command? Who helps us?

Read 2 Corinthians 5:10

What does this verse say about choices we make to follow God's plan?

Prayer: Father, reveal to me those areas I need to deny myself so that I may seek first Your kingdom. Give me strength to pursue Your will and good pleasure without hesitation or restraint. Jesus, I thank You for your sacrifice and how it changed my life and destiny, and I praise You for this changed heart. In Jesus' name. Amen.

Activation: Take time to ask God what 'seeking the kingdom' looks like. Ask how you can seek, and write down your thoughts in your journal. Purpose to apply those principles to your life over the next month.

Take Up Your Cross

My beloved [shepherd] is to me a cluster of henna flowers in the vineyards of En-gedi.

The Song of Solomon 1:14

Again the bride enjoys the pleasure of rest, this time in the vineyards of En-gedi. The lush oasis along the Dead Sea contained many natural springs of water and was within the territory of the tribe of Judah. It was not only a place of rest but for David a place to hide from the pursuit of King Saul. The name En-gedi means the fountain of the lamb.

The prophet Ezekiel 47:1-13 speaks of the future of this oasis. The river of life, which flows from the temple, will spill over the land, bringing nourishment and life to the desert. It will flow into the Dead Sea and heal its waters, purging it of all its waste, and the village of En-gedi will be the place from which many cast their fishing nets. This river of life flows from the temple and Jesus states; "Now on the last and most important day of the feast, Jesus stood and called out [in a loud voice], "If anyone is thirsty, let him come to Me and drink! 38 He who believes in Me [who adheres to, trusts in, and relies on Me], as the Scripture has said, 'From his innermost being will flow continually rivers of living water." John 7:37-38

The beloved Shepherd in the vineyard is compared to the henna blooms. Pure white and highly fragrant they were prized for perfumes, but if one were to bruise a henna leaf they would find it bleeds a crimson stain on the skin. Our beloved bridegroom is pure rest, and His blood washes us with an anointing perfume.

Where do you rest when the cares of the world weigh you down?

Read Isaiah 5:7

What is this 'house' and how can it be a vineyard?

Read Isaiah 27:1-3

What happens to the serpent? What has the Lord done for His 'chosen vineyard'?

Prayer: Thank You Lord for the springs of water that flow from Your throne. I pray that You fill me to overflowing in this place of rest so that I might share this rest with others.

Activation: Many of us have a place we rest or get away from the burdens we carry. Does your place of rest point you toward God? Take some time to turn your resting place into a place you're pointed toward Him. Add a Bible, some scripture verses in frames, or a speaker there to play worship music. You'll find your rest more fulfilling when God is present and welcomed.

Eyes Fixed On The King

Behold, you are beautiful, my love! Behold, you are beautiful! You have doves' eyes.

The Song of Solomon 1:15

The double praises of the king toward her external beauty are nothing compared to the beautiful eyes of a dove. The Holy Spirit was with Jesus during his ministry on earth, but this same Holy Spirit now resides within all believers for the purpose of revealing Jesus to us.

This dove was sent by Noah to search if the waters had receded from the land. The Spirit was with God in the beginning, hovering over the waters, and the Spirit was again present over the waters of this renewal. Twice it was sent and eventually returned with an olive branch.

This dove, while searching over all the waters covering the land, found the symbol of the Prince of Peace, of our redemption, and of our High Priest.

To have the eyes of the dove one must open their eyes to the revelation of Jesus, to His priestly ministry in our lives, to His work of redemption, and to His perfect peace. It was only through His sacrifice that this same Holy Spirit was made available to all believers. Our eyes must be fixed on Him just like the eyes of the dove.

Read John 8:12

What will all who focus on Jesus have?

Read Hosea 14:5-7

What is Jesus compared to in these verses? What do those who dwell under His shadow receive?

Read John 16:14

Who does the Holy Spirit reveal to believers?

Read Matthew 3:16

The Holy Spirit 'lighted' on Jesus after His baptism. Why was this important?

Prayer: Thank You Jesus that You have given me the light of life. I pray this light would illuminate what lies before me that I may walk without stumbling and overcome any obstacles the enemy sets before me. Thank You for Your blessed rest and peace. In Jesus' name. Amen.

Activation: With your journal open in front of you ask the Holy Spirit to reveal Jesus to you. Write down all you hear.

He Is Worthy

Behold, you are beautiful, my beloved [shepherd], yes, delightful! Our arbor and couch are green and leafy.

The Song of Solomon 1:16

What can this bride to be do other than praise her bridegroom for these gifts and graces? All things are secondary to His perfect rest. Knowing Him is paramount and where better to sense the heart of the King than where He relaxes? This covered couch was the place of rest during the heat of the day for kings and queens, but this couch is not of metal or wood. Instead it is alive and flourishing.

While the building of the temple adorned wood and stone with precious jewels, the bride of Christ is the temple herself. This living temple where the Holy Spirit resides gives honor and praise to the Father daily. It is His workmanship on display to the world and the work of Jesus on display in its full restoration.

What is the significance of a living resting place? How is this different than the temple building?

Psalm 23:2
Where does the Lord lead us and bring us to rest?

Read Jeramiah 17:7-8

What promises are given to those who trust in the Lord's leading?

Prayer: I praise you Father for making me a temple of the Holy Spirit. Lead and guide me into all truth and continue to reveal to me Your will and Word.

Activation: Take the time to worship the Lord today. I highly suggest the song "Take Me In" by Catherine Mullins.

A Solid Foundation

The beams of our house are cedars, and our rafters and panels are cypresses or pines.

The Song of Solomon 1:17

The cedars of Lebanon were the most often used trees in any large structure of the day. They grow to substantial heights and are perfectly upright. They were used in the building of the temple having been hewn to measure and placed around the inner court. This natural temple was built on the foundation of costly stone. Now our foundation is in Christ with Jesus as the chief corner stone (Mark 12:10).

This temple, built by the Lord's sacrifice and indwelt by the Holy Spirit, is now perfectly upright by the righteousness of Christ Jesus. The inner sanctuary was home of the Ark of the Covenant and is now the heart of the believer, with the law written upon our hearts instead of on tablets of stone. The roots of the trees run deep into the waters of life He provides and grow toward heavenly knowledge.

Define Righteousness:

How are we made righteous?

Read 2 Corinthians 3:3

How does the law written on hearts differ from one written on stone?

Read Psalm 118:2

Who are the builders? Why did the reject the cornerstone?

Prayer: I praise You Lord that this living temple is set apart and holy by Your sacrifice. I pray that You reveal this law written on my heart as I read Your word and worship You in spirit and truth.

Activation: God is always speaking, and with the inward Holy Spirit we can hear Him clearly. It's often an exercise in practice and patience. Take time today to simply sit with the Father and listen. Write down any thoughts or ideas that come to mind, or if a scripture sticks out to you. He may be telling you something important about work or your family.

CHAPTER 2

In My Weakness, He is Strong

His Love Covers

[She said] I am only a little rose or autumn crocus of the Plain of Sharon, or a [humble]
lily of the valleys [that grows in deep and difficult places].

The Song of Solomon 2:1

The word translated "rose" is really חֲבַצֶּלֶת chabatstseleth. It is a word we see nowhere else in scripture. The roots of this word are "habab", which is used only once in Deuteronomy 33:3, meaning God's sense of love for His people, and "salal" meaning to shadow. This word can be translated as God's love overshadowing.

It's because of His great love for us He sent Jesus as our redeemer from sin. We grow upon the Plain of Sharon overshadowed by His great love. The Plain of Sharon lies between Mount Carmel in the north and Joppa to the south in the region of Samaria. Its name denotes a fruitful place, and it was the territory of the tribe of Manasseh, who was the oldest son of Joseph.

There are many meanings hidden within the name Manassah that illuminate the redemptive works of Jesus. It can mean; to 'lift up' one's hands, feet, or head, to bear or carry a burden, to take or take away from, one who is lifted up, the lifted up utterance of an oracle or prophet. Even while her heart cries because she is cursed to live in this ungodly world because of mans' fall, the bride understands her need to be under the watchful gaze and care of her shepherd in this fertile plain he tends.

Along the Plain of Sharon's northern border we find Mount Caramel which divides this lush fertile plain from the Valley of Megiddo. The Hebrew word כרמל karmel means a vineyard or orchard, but it also denotes in its many variations the one who tends or dresses a vineyard. Again we see our bridegroom acting as our mediator and advocate separating the lushness of the promise from the valley of judgment.

The alabaster-colored lilies found in the south of this region grow several feet tall and bloom both day and night. During the evening and night, the perfume from these lilies grows in strength and sweetness. The choicest of these grew in the valleys close to the running brooks which fed the fertile soils on the plain.

The word lily refers to the trumpet shape of the flower which grows upon a tall stem. Though the lily grows to great heights, its flower head hangs as though showing its beauty and strength but humbling itself as our bridegroom did when He took on human flesh.

This bride is right to focus on the overshadowing of the Father's love. We must understand while we still sin and fall short of the glory of God, He no longer sees us in this way. Now we are viewed through the blood of Jesus, which cleansed us of all unrighteousness. Just as this Plain of Sharon is divided from the valley of judgment we too are set apart and free to live with reborn spirits.

Why do you feel it's necessary to be at peace as we grow in faith?

Read Genesis 3:17-18 and Matthew 13:22

What do these thorns represent?

Read Hebrews 6:7-8

What should we do with these thorns if we see them in our lives?

Read Psalm 103:12

Why is it necessary that God remove our transgressions?

Matthew 20:28

How has this verse changed in meaning or depth with what you have just learned?

Prayer: I praise You Lord that Your love overshadows me today. I pray that You always speak of who I am in Christ, and help me to see myself the way You see me. Thank You I am separated from judgement unto Christ. In Jesus' name. Amen.

Activation: In your journal write down all the ways you are now free in Christ. Ask the Lord how you can share this wonderful freedom with someone today.

Come Out From Among Them

But Solomon replied, "Like the lily among thorns, so are you, my love, among the daughters."

The Song of Song 2:2

Again the sweet and fragrant lilies are mentioned, this time describing the bride. Her purity of heart in her pursuit of Him sets her apart from the others. To be white as snow we must be washed in the blood of the lamb.

How can one so pure and lovely grow among the thorns? Again, the daughters of Jerusalem are mentioned, and they are compared to the thorns of the field. The robust thorns take root and spring up quickly, growing large enough to smother anything under them. To pluck them out of place is challenging and often one endures scratches and punctures. Jesus gives us the example of one sown among thorns in the Gospel of Matthew (13:22)

How vexing for the bride to be told she is still among the thorns. Cares of the world in any believer's life will slowly choke the lush, rich growth God so fervently desires. He compares her to the lily, radiant and pure, washed white as snow, but her old life and old way of thinking have yet to die away completely.

The lily is unique in many ways. Few flowers are taller, and even fewer grow more fragrant as night descends. The lily also yields an incredible number of seed pods per flower head. Several species of lily found growing in the region produce fifty or more pods. The Lord is making a point to her that she is utterly unique.

While we stand in the midst of the sinful world, we are called to be pillars of righteousness. The bride must prune and tend her heart in order for the Word to take root in her heart. Once this Word takes root and begins to grow we must not allow the cares of this world to overtake our thoughts.

Have you ever written off worry or anxiety in your life? What caused it? What made you overlook it?

Read Isaiah 1:18
Explain the spiritual significance of being 'white as snow'.

Read Revelation 19:7-8
How are the fine linen garments described in these verses?

Read Matthew 13:22-23

What is the difference between the soil condition of those in the thorns and those who produce fruit? Why is this so important?

Read Romans 12:2

What do you think 'renewing your mind' means? What are some ways you can renew your mind to Christ?

Prayer: Thank You Lord that I have the mind of Christ. All the worries and cares of this world are in Your hand, and I rest in knowing You care for me and have the best planned for me. I praise You that I am called righteous by Your sacrifice. Help me see the areas I need to rely on You and trust You more. In Jesus' name. Amen.

Activation: Any gardener will tell you thorns are pesky. We can weed and pull, then weed and pull some more, but often the roots run deep. Many times we don't even understand why thoughts, anxieties, or cares of this life keep returning. With your journal open take time today to ask God about any thorns in your life that keep coming back. Ask Him for His solution to those 'roots' in your life, and write down what you hear. His overshadowing love desires you to be free in all areas of your life.

Under The Shadow

Like an apple tree among the trees of the wood, so is my beloved [shepherd] among the sons [cried the girl]! Under his shadow I delighted to sit, and his fruit was sweet to my taste.

The Song of Solomon 2:3

Just as the bride arrayed in white is a beautiful sight to her Redeemer, He stands out from all the others in her sights. There are many trees lovely to our sights, but they bear no fruit for the Lord's kingdom. They gather and array themselves with superficial ornaments which cast shade on those trying to spring up under them.

While the thorns choke out my crowding, the heavy shade cast in the woods chokes the precious sunlight before it ever reaches the saplings. While it may be easy to live under the shadow of these trees of the wood, who seemingly take all the heat of the sun and the brunt of winds, no one can ever thrive in this place for long without the light.

It is under this much more pleasant shade the bride wishes to rest and abide. This rest is a relief from her previous toil under the sun where she was exposed to the ideas and culture of man. Here she is near her Shepherd and can take hold of His fruits which are pleasant for the palate.

As we enjoy this partaking of the first fruits which is Christ, we partake in the celebration of His resurrection and ascension to glory at the right hand of God. The Fruits of the Spirit are produced in our lives as we rest and rely on the faithfulness of our bridegroom and grow in our relationship to Him. Our growth in Him is a progression like the one the bride has so far enjoyed.

First she exclaimed He was so wonderful she would run after Him, and this fervent running slowed to a close following. Now she sits and rests. While our lives as believers often move at differing paces in various seasons of life one must remember that to endure a race is to pace yourself so you reach your destination (Is 40:31).

Have you grown weary running after God? What have you learned so far in this study that has changed your pursuit of Him?

Read Proverbs 25:11

Describe how these apples are similar to the apples the maiden partakes of under the tree.

Read Isaiah 25:4 and Psalm 121:5-8

What is available to those who dwell under God's shadow?

Read 1 Cor. 15:23

What does it mean that Christ is the 'first fruits' of those that would come later?

Read Philippians 1:10-12 in the Amplified

Write this verse in your own words.

Prayer: Thank You Jesus that You were the first fruit and that through You I am righteous. Help me develop these fruits of the spirit that I might help glorify the Father and bring the lost to Christ. I praise You Father that it's under Your shadow that I find rest and comfort. In Jesus' name. Amen.

Activation: Read Galatians 5:22-23 and list the Fruits of the Spirit. Beside each fruit write out how you see it in your life today. Are there any you lack or don't feel are fully developed? Take time to ask God what you can do to develop this fruit.

A Song of Joy

He brought me to the banqueting house, and his banner over me was love [for love waved as a protecting and comforting banner over my head when I was near him].

The Song of Songs 2:4

As we partake of the fruit our bridegroom provides we glimpse the extent He provides for us as believers. He brought us to the banqueting house as prized guests on whom He lavishes His presence. It is the celebration of newness of life in Him and our full redemption from sin and death. We see all things are new and we are redeemed by His sacrifice.

This banquet house is not just the place of wine and celebration, but this house contains the vessels of new wine of the new and better covenant found in Him. This blood sacrifice foreshadowed by the daily wine offering in the temple brings us again to an understanding that all things in Him are new.

We cannot in any way think of Jesus with an old mindset and we cannot change our future by focusing on our past. To think in an old mindset would say I am a sinner, but with our bridegroom, we can now say I am redeemed. This redemption is done once and for all, and His banner waves over us as a covering of love.

A banner or standard in Solomon's time gave people notice of who was approaching. It distinguished if a group was friendly and allowed to enter the gates, or if the fighting men of the city would be called to defend it. This banner over us is Christ's standard of love. It distinguishes who He is to us and allows us to lower our defenses so He may enter.

What does it mean to you to be considered a prized guest? How would you react to a host of a party who gave you a special honor?

Read Psalm 5:7

How do we enter the Lord's house?

Read Psalm 60:4-5

What does this banner protect us from?

Prayer: Thank You Lord for inviting me to the banquet hall. Help me know You more and fully understand the banner of love You've set over me. Lord, help me renew my mind and set aside my old way of thinking so that I may follow You as Your disciple. In Jesus' name. Amen.

Activation: Imagine this banner of love. What do you think it looks like? Draw a representation of the banner of love in your journal. Make sure you include yourself! This banner is over you now.

All I Need

Sustain me with raisins; refresh me with apples, for I am sick with love.

The Song of Songs 2:5

Cakes of raisins and fruits are not foods one finds in the banquet halls of earthly kings. There one would find succulent feasts and an array of choice meats, but the bride notices it is not the gorging of her flesh that will sustain her. Pure fruit provided to us from the one who is the vine and tree of life will cause newness to spring up in us. This new life feeds on the joy and love of the Father.

The love of the Father is greater than anything we can know or comprehend, and as we progress on this journey of betrothal to our bridegroom we gain further glimpses into His heart. As we know and understand more and more His love for us we are overcome in our hearts with His grace, mercy, and love.

This progression is mentioned by Paul in 2 Corinthians 3 when he instructs the church to behold Christ. As we look to Him we are then transformed into His image, but the progression of glory is incremental. While we are born again, it takes time for the Fruits of the Spirit to grow and become evident in our lives. This period of growth or sickness of love may seem agonizing, but our desire to be more like Christ is our motivation to continue down the path of discipleship.

Sickness comes in many forms and here we find a sickness of love. To understand the love of the Father we must see the weakness of our flesh to comprehend it. The word חָלָה challah translated "sickness" literally means to wear through, become weak, or rub until raw. This weakness or wounding of our flesh is so slight in comparison to the wounds of our bridegroom.

He bore them for us, understanding that His strength made available to us is how we overcome our weakness. When we are faced with our own inability to earn right standing with the Father, and the obvious grace of Christ's sacrifice, we find ourselves needing more of the fruits of this great vine, the strength He provides, and the shade and rest of one who is the tree of life.

Have you felt worn or sick with love during your time as a believer?

Read Acts 3:20-21

What are the two promises for those who are in the Lord's presence?

Read Psalm 123:2-3

What is the promise for those who wait upon the Lord? Describe what you think waiting upon the Lord means.

Prayer: I praise You Lord that You know the end from the beginning. All my days are known to You and You have provided a place of rest and refreshing for all of them. I thank You that as I focus on Your word and truth and grow in the fruit of patience I will grow from glory to glory. Help me to show the world Your glory. In Jesus' name. Amen.

Activation: In your journal you wrote down the fruits of the spirit and how you felt they had developed in your life. Take the fruit you feel is most developed so far and think back to when you first made Jesus Lord. Write down your thoughts about how far you've come thanking God for your progress so far. Your testimony of growth in character will encourage others. Be ready to share!

By His Hand

[I can feel] His left hand under my head and his right hand embraces me!

The Song of Songs 2:6

The loving embrace of our bridegroom shows the willingness of our Savior to embrace us. These same hands, which bore the nail holes, embrace not only our heads but also our hearts. The sacrifice of our King was not only for our spirits to again be alive in Him, but also to redeem us to dominion and authority on the earth.

This authority grants us rights and privileges unavailable to unbelievers, such as the inward Holy Spirit and the use of Jesus' name. The Spirit within us makes us alive to God again, and we are embraced by His strong arm. The strong arm of the Lord is what brings victory to the children of Israel in battle. Here it is embracing the bride because it was His sacrifice and desire for intimacy that delivered her. We are able to rest in this assurance of our already secured victory in Christ.

The left hand is supporting the head of the bride. It's the hand of supplication and surrender. Our minds that are often the battlefield the enemy chooses to engage us on. Many believers live life in a state of defeat because they allow the enemy free reign into their minds. It is why Paul tells us time and time again to renew our minds and to take thoughts captive to the obedience of Christ. Surrendering our minds to His Lordship keeps us free to pursue every good work without distraction.

The enemy uses feelings of defeat and hopelessness to keep us deceived and blinded to the truth of who God is. Many times the Father is viewed as distant and a judging taskmaster reigning from distant heaven, but the truth is He is the Father from whom all good things flow. While Satan would accuse us of past wrongs and make us feel inadequate, we must remember the loving embrace of our bridegroom offers us rest from the heat of trials and accusations.

How would you describe renewing your mind? Do you find yourself battling negative thoughts regularly?

Read Rev 3:21

What does the right hand of God represent? Who sits there now?

Read Luke 10:19

How might this verse help you with your thoughts?

Read Romans 8:6

What can you do to develop the mind of peace instead of the flesh?

Read Hebrews 4:3

How easy is it to enter into the Lord's rest? What do you feel keeps you from resting in Him?

Prayer: Lord, I rest in Your embrace now and thank You for Your goodness and mercy. I ask that You help me renew my mind to the authority I have in Christ. Let my words speak Your will on earth as in Heaven. In Jesus' name. Amen.

Application: In Matthew 10:1-8 Jesus speaks to His disciples and tasks them with the work of the Kingdom. In your journal write down all Jesus called the disciples to do. Ask the Father for an opportunity to do His kingdom work and rely on the Holy Spirit to work miracles through you!

Surrender to Rest

[He said] I charge you, O you daughters of Jerusalem, by the gazelles or by the hinds of the field [which are free to follow their own instincts] that you not try to stir up or awaken [my] love until it pleases.

The Song of Songs 2:7

This perfect rest the bridegroom offers none can interfere. He commands these cares, whether they are circumstances or people, with the penalty of a curse to not cause agitation or worry. These cares of the world that the enemy would try to tempt us with, in order that we would leave the loving embrace of our King, do not even rouse a response in us for this rest is sacred.

Though we are to pursue our bridegroom with our whole heart, it's necessary to know that love matures at its own pace. As believers, we should never stir up unhealthy pursuits in others. It is the maturity of each individual believer, and the walk in which they take, that allows this perfect love to grow to its full measure.

It is often the opinions of others that cause us to stir ourselves up and try to perform for the Father. It is important that we support the path of each believer by allowing this love and intimacy to mature at its own pace. It's through an intimate relationship with the Father that we find what we are to do as individuals.

How would you describe surrendering to rest in the Lord?

Read Psalm 46:8

Describe striving in your own words. Are there areas in your life you've been striving? How might you surrender these to God?

Read Hebrews 4:10

What does this verse tell us about the importance of rest?

Read Exodus 13:13-14

What key points do you see in this verse?

Prayer: Thank You Lord for this blessed rest. I praise You for Your love and kindness toward me, and I thank You for taking all my cares and worries. Help me see myself as You see me. Help me to overcome the need to please others before You. In Jesus' name. Amen.

Activation: Write down all the things you have been striving toward. Take those things and with a shout of joy tear them up! Jesus took all our burdens so that we would cease from striving. Thank Him for taking those burdens from you. Be aware that you don't start picking them up again. The first sign is usually beginning to think about them often. If this happens, thank Him again, you aren't carrying them anymore. Let's defeat the enemy in our minds with the Word of Truth.

Hear His Voice

[Vividly she pictured it] The voice of my beloved [shepherd]! Behold, he comes, leaping upon the mountains, bounding over the hills.

The Song of Songs 2:8

A most beautiful picture as our bride to be notices she does in fact hear the voice of her Shepherd. It is the promise to all believers that we can know the voice of Jesus (John 10:27). It is often in this place of rest, where all worries, cares, and thoughts of the world are silenced that we hear Him first and best.

Stillness within our hearts and minds is necessary to hear and recognize the voice of our Shepherd. He comes leaping upon mountains and bounding over hills in His zealous joy, but to hear His voice we must understand rest and stillness. It is a stillness Elijah learned in the desert of Horeb, also known as Sinai.

In 1 Kings 18, Elijah defeated the prophets of Baal when fire rained down from heaven and consumed the offering on Mt. Carmel. When he learned of Jezebel's anger and desire to kill him, he fled to Beersheba where he sat under a juniper tree and prayed that he might die. We must ask ourselves how one could win a contest with 400 pagan prophets, then wish death just days later. Elijah cries out to God, and His answer is one that illuminates much to every believer.

"So he got up and ate and drank, and with the strength of that food he traveled forty days and nights to Horeb (Sinai), the mountain of God." 1 Kings 19:8 AMP

When Elijah reaches the mountain, he rests and when he wakes, the Lord asks him a shocking question, "What are you doing here, Elijah?" Certainly, he must be annoyed, as one would expect God to know our thoughts and plans. He knew Elijah had traveled to this place in the wilderness. Elijah's response is familiar to many believers when faced with opposition from the world.

"He said, "I have been very zealous for the Lord God of hosts (armies), because the sons of Israel have abandoned (broken) Your covenant, torn down Your altars and killed Your prophets with the sword. And I, only I, am left; and they seek to take away my life." 1 Kings 19:10 AMP

Righteous anger was Elijah's response. He is telling God, I'm here because of you, but he misses the greater question posed. Why was he in the wilderness, when God had a plan and purpose for him in Israel? Elijah was never instructed by the Lord to flee Mt. Carmel after the defeat of the prophets of Baal. Instead he fled out of fear for what Jezebel and her men would do if they captured him.

Fear is a powerful force that is in direct opposition to the power of faith. Where faith is belief and trust in God, fear is faith and trust in the devil, and it can drive new and mature believers away from their purpose and destiny.

Throughout his life, Elijah experienced the supernatural favor and deliverance only the Father could bring, but he was still a man with human faults. All can fall into the trap of believing what our eyes see, without weighing the truth that the Spirit within us is greater. God's lesson for Elijah is one we all must learn.

"So He said, 'Go out and stand on the mountain before the Lord.' And behold, the Lord was passing by, and a great and powerful wind was tearing out the mountains and breaking the rocks in pieces before the Lord; but the Lord was not in the wind. And after the wind, [there was] an earthquake, but the Lord was not in the earthquake. 12 After the earthquake, [there was] a fire, but the Lord was not in the fire; and after the fire, [there was] the sound of a gentle blowing." 1 Kings 19:11-12 AMP

While the King James renders this last verse as 'a still small voice', the proper literal translation from Hebrew reads 'a voice in fragile silence'. Silence is as varied as the world. Silence in nature can include anything from wind rustling through trees, to the sound of crickets in the deep of night, but here in the wilderness, it is a desert silence. One where you may hear the scurry of a beetle in the sand, or the cry of a hawk miles in the sky. It is a silence that renders any sound loud and clear. The Lord speaks clearly if we are willing to hear and listen.

Again the Lord questions Elijah, but in a different way, as this second verse properly reads from the Hebrew, "What is here for you Elijah?" There are no prophets of Baal or wayward Israelites for him to chastise and elicit his righteous anger upon. Nearly dying in his desire to crawl back to this mountain of law and stone, Elijah faces the Lord's difficult question. Is this mountain of law where he would prefer to lie down and die, with pride as his companion? Does he still wish to be used as a servant in a place of humble obedience? It's a question we must all face.

Who are we here? Within the rest of our bridegroom's embrace, we understand this simple truth, we are His. In all that He wishes us to do, let us see Him leaping with joy as we hear His voice. Let us know the rest only He can provide so that we might wake to newness and run our course, whether it brings us over mountains or hills. Let us follow His leading and direction from a place of humility and obedience. Trust in the Lord for He is good.

Have you ever run in fear from a person or circumstance? Why did you flee?

Would your actions have changed if you listened to the Holy Spirit?

Read John 10:4

What is the promise of this verse? How does it apply to you?

Read Psalm 22

What is the title of this Psalm? What are the promises of this Psalm?

Prayer: Lord, I thank You that in every circumstance and every place I hear Your voice clearly. Thank you for the plan that has been set before me, and thank You for going before me. Thank you that under Your shadow and by Your strength I am able to overcome fear and worry. Help me see myself as an overcomer. I praise You that I rest in this cleft of the rock and grow closer to You. In Jesus' name. Amen.

Activation: Many of our activation exercises have involved your journal. Today we will begin using more prophetic actions. What is a prophetic act? Throughout scripture we see individuals making declarations or performing actions that lead to a breakthrough in situations or relationships. The children of Israel were led by God to circle the city of Jericho. The walk didn't bring down the walls, but the action in obedience led to supernatural victory. Rising up in authority in Christ is understanding we must move in all the gifts of the Spirit, and through these prophetic acts you'll learn to discern the Holy Spirit's leading.

Fear causes many to run from the will of God. We face the enemy and it gets overwhelming. Today you're going to think about what you've run from recently. Open your journal to the banner of love you drew earlier. Imagining the fear, begin waving the banner over your head and proclaim that God is faithful to accomplish His will. Tell the enemy you won't be fearing him anymore. Make an effort today to move back into alignment with God's will and see Him move mightily on your behalf.

Make Room for the King

My beloved is like a gazelle or a young hart. Behold, he stands behind the wall of our house, he looks in through the windows, he glances through the lattice.

The Song of Songs 2:9

While the bride shows great progress in her attentiveness to the Holy Spirit, it is an important reminder that our bridegroom desires us. While He stands within sight of her, one must notice He is outside the walls. How can this be when she says it is 'our' house? Didn't she invite His presence into her very chamber?

He peers through these windows to her soul as though He is an outsider. While His presence had been invited in, one must wonder if the room was ever made for Him. What could possibly keep this bride to be from making room? Jesus tells us in the parable of the dinner guests (Luke 14:16-24)

All these auspicious guests had been invited by the man to dinner and were expected when it was ready. Once they were told all was ready, we see each one makes excuses as to why they could not attend. While the invitation was inviting, once they realized it meant forgoing other things, they learned the true cost of following Jesus was higher than they were willing to pay.

Many profess their love and desire to sit and commune with the King of Kings, but few follow through with their profession. It is the nature of our flesh to reject the things of God, but we must know and understand that we are new creations in Christ. Our profession must be sincere, and to make room for Him, we must set aside the sin of self.

Each excuse given by these guests is rooted in some self-interest. Whether it be in Self-Importance, Self-Sufficiency, or Self-Indulgence, all are obstacles to allowing ourselves freedom to follow Jesus. Conforming to the example of Jesus is a test to our flesh and of our will. At its root, the sin of selfishness is lifting ourselves above the place where God put us.

While we are sons and daughters of the Father, we must understand that our lives are no longer our own. All believers are called to live in accordance with His word, and only the

Father should occupy first place in our lives. Anything that is allowed in His place is something we allow ourselves to see as provider, comforter, or security in His place.

Have you given any excuses to God why you can't do something?

Have you made room for Jesus in your daily life? What ways have you found it easiest to invite Him in? Are there any places you've found it difficult to invite Him in?

Read 1 Samuel 6:6

In what ways do you harden your heart to the Word or Will of God? Why?

Read Luke 14:16-24

What do you think are the implications of turning down the dinner invitation?

Read Revelation 19:8-9

Who is invited to this dinner? Who attends?

Read-Galatians 1:10

Who do we seek to please as believers? Why can we not seek the praise of men?

Prayer: Lord, help me overcome selfishness in my life. Let me live fully for You in my heart and mind, and help me overcome the desire to please anyone but You. I thank You that as I focus on Your word and make room for You in all that I do, I am changed. In Jesus' name. Amen.

Activation: Changing habits can be difficult without reminders. Ask the Lord today how you can remind yourself to seek Him first in every situation. Should you put a reminder on your phone or maybe a background image? Maybe a WWJD bracelet would help remind you. Whatever God shows you to do, find a way to incorporate it every day for a week. Journal what happens and share it with us! @discipleshiptr1 on twitter.

Wherever You Go

My beloved speaks and says to me, Rise up, my love, my fair one, and come away.

The Song of Songs 2:10

Just as Jesus called to the disciples and said 'Follow Me', we see this very same invitation given to the bride. In order to follow where He leads us it is necessary that we rise up and come away from the places we know and are comfortable in. For the disciples, it was following Him away from family and provision.

For each of the disciples it was the beginning of walking alongside the Savior and experiencing the miracles and wonders He performed. It was the beginning of intimacy with the One who is the bread of life. Discipleship with Jesus was not a stale endurance of endless and lifeless lessons, but vibrant teaching by example in the midst of a hurting people.

He still calls us to discipleship today. For some it is the literal laying down of their lives for the gospel, and for many others, it can mean the estrangement or disdain of those they care for.

The disregard we must show for the opinions of others contrary to the word is not meant to incite their anger or resentment, instead it is meant to show our obedience to the Father and the leading of His Holy Spirit. In Ephesians 4:15 Paul tells us to share all truth wrapped in love. This loss of self-consciousness is our sure sign that the roots related to selfishness and pride are being plucked from our lives.

It is by His righteousness and His faithfulness that we are empowered to do the work of the kingdom. If we lose sight of the necessity of Jesus at the center of all we do, those works become the wood, hay, and stubble burned up on that day of Christ's judgment. To do the work of the kingdom outside the comfort and rest of Jesus, we soon find ourselves drained and depleted.

While Jesus often spoke of the need for all disciples to follow His example, one that is often hardest is the need for all to rest in Him. The church as a body is charged with preaching to the lost and demonstrating His might and power with signs, wonders, and miracles, but we must remember from whom all these blessings flow.

How often do we see believers, especially pastors and leaders, working to the point of anger, frustration, and exhaustion? This was never the plan of the Father or of Jesus, for He often reminded the apostles to rest and remove themselves from the field of work to seek Him.

Do you see yourself as a disciple of Jesus? Why or Why not?

Read Luke 14:25-35

How would you define being a disciple of Christ?

Read Mark 6:30

What does this verse teach us about rest while doing kingdom work?

Prayer: I praise You Lord that I've been called to walk with You. I thank You for leading me and guiding me in all things. Let my life be a testimony to Your goodness and grace. I ask that You strengthen me through Your Spirit and help me know and understand when I need to rest. In Jesus' name. Amen.

Application: Is there anything you're reluctant to leave? Maybe you're reluctant to leave a person, a job, or home. Following Jesus isn't easy when we are given a task that causes us discomfort. The good news is He is always with us. Ask the Lord what He has for you to do, and write down everything you hear. Ask the Lord for help with the anxiety or stress that might come if you are asked to go anywhere or change a part of your life. You may also find He already has you right where He wants you to be. Whether you're called to a mission trip, a job change, or to remain faithful where you are, expect exciting things with Jesus.

Glory to Glory

For, behold, the winter is past; the rain is over and gone.

The Song of Songs 2:11

The time spent in winter, while we put down deeper roots into the things of God, soon comes to an end as He reminds us this time is not permanent. Periods of growth and establishment during our rest are always followed by the rains of spring. They soak deep and quicken new life to burst forth and grow.

The blooms of spring are not for the tree itself, but rather they are for others to partake from. As we grow in the knowledge of God and seek His face, we begin to understand the need for sharing that which we received from Him. When we have rested and refreshed ourselves in Him, the truth of our newness in Christ overtakes our thoughts as we find ourselves yearning for this time of fruitfulness.

This rain that brings forth new growth is called the winter rain. It falls on the land of Israel during the months of December to March, and there is often no stretch of fair weather during this time. It is why the Israelites refer to winter as 'the dark season'. To many, the necessity of rains in season is lost, but to the people of this day, it was essential rain fell during the correct times (Leviticus 26:3-4).

During the wintertime rains, crops previously planted enjoy the constant supply of water that allows them to reach full maturity. Later in the spring, the rains are more subtle and the grains swell to full maturity for harvest. To have rains out of season within this normally arid region of the world would spell a failed harvest and famine in the land. It was the purpose of these rains to bring full and abundant harvest of fruit.

The Father created this natural world; its rhythm of seasons, fruit, and harvest teaches us many things about spiritual truth. Fruits of the Spirit grow in us as we seek His face and read the Word. The nourishment it provides our soul and spirit keep us focused on this great work of discipleship and intimacy with Him.

Think about your life in Christ. Have there been times you've felt you needed a refreshing? How did you notice you needed a refreshing?

Read Isaiah 45:8

To what is this rain likened? Why is this significant for believers?

Read Hosea 6:3

How will the Lord come? Explain why you think this allegory is significant.

Read Acts 14:17

What is the effect of rain in this verse? How does this apply to your life?

Prayer: I praise you Lord that I am fruitful. As I look to You, let all the fruits of the Spirit grow in me so that I may bless others with Your goodness, grace, and mercy. Let my life be a beacon and hope for those who don't know you, or who are questioning your goodness. In Jesus' name. Amen.

Activation: One of the most important things to remember about sharing the fruits of the spirit with anyone is the necessity to share in meaningful ways they understand. Your best helper is the Holy Spirit. He knows everyone and their needs. As you go about your day, remember to ask the Holy Spirit to lead and guide you to people who need joy, peace, or patience. You have been actively cultivating these fruits in your life. Now is the time to watch how God uses you to share them with others.

This Kingdom Work

The flowers appear on the earth; the time of the singing [of birds] has come, and the voice of the turtledove is heard in our land.

The Song of Songs 2:12

After this deepening of our roots into the person of Jesus through the Word, we see new life springing up. The flowers of the field that our bridegroom called out are now growing with abundance. Jesus shows us here that even before we see the flowers or fruits of righteousness we must call them out of others. Many times it is the speaking of those things in faith that produces their appearance in our lives (Hebrews 11).

This voice of the turtledove heard throughout the land is the heart of bridegroom. His voice is calling all believers to a time of growth and abundance through relationship with Him.

The flowers that blossom in springtime are the birthplaces of fruit which carries the seed, which perpetuates the cycle of seedtime and harvest.

This seed that is grown in our heart represents the truth of the Word that has taken root in our hearts. To tend this precious soil, we must remove those ideas from the world and replace them with the truths found in the Word. Once these truths begin to flourish and multiply in our own lives, the necessity of sowing into others becomes clear. Fruit is never consumed by the tree which grows it. The fruitfulness of our lives can and will produce faith and hope in others as they witness the transformation that only God can bring.

Our testimony is more than the words we speak to encourage others to the new life found in Christ. It is a life lived in surrender to the Father's will and good pleasure, and a willingness to share our abundance of joy, peace, and hope with those who have none.

How have you been actively removing the world's ideas from your heart and mind? Do you see a difference in your thought life? Do you see a difference in your emotions?

Read Proverbs 18:21

How might one speak death? How can we speak life? What are the implications of each to the one who's speaking?

Read Psalm 97:11 in the Amplified

What is the light sewn? What happens when you sew it?

Read Hebrews 11:3

How does faith create hope and life based on this verse?

Prayer: Thank you Lord that as I've renewed my mind to who I am in Christ, Your voice has become clearer to me. I thank you that in all things I can overcome and renew my dedication to this life of discipleship. In Jesus' name. Amen.

Activation: Today I'd like you to review your testimony in your journal. Is there anything you'd like to add? Maybe you've had a great breakthrough since you began following this study, or you've seen an answer to prayer. It's important to remember that our lives in Christ are always deepening and we are always growing. This means the testimony we share may change. Even if it doesn't, it's still a good time to think about the new things you've experienced with Him. Praise Him!

Arise, My Love

The fig tree puts forth and ripens her green figs, and the vines are in blossom and give forth their fragrance. Arise, my love, my fair one, and come away.

The Song of Songs 2:13

The Bible is a story of trees. The first two being the tree of life and the tree of the knowledge of good and evil, both of which grew in the midst of the Garden of Eden. Every tree was made available to Adam and Eve except the tree of the knowledge of good and evil. When they had eaten the fruit and realized they were naked, they sewed fig leaves together, and this mention of figs brings to light an interesting correlation we see later in the book of Jeremiah.

Then the Lord said to me, 'What do you see, Jeremiah?' And I said, 'Figs, the good figs, very good; and the bad figs, very bad, so rotten that they cannot be eaten.' Jeremiah 24:3 AMP

We are told these good figs are those Israelites who followed the Lord into captivity in Babylon. They followed the direction of the Lord and were saved as a remnant of people to return to the land of promise. These evil figs were the officials and king Zedekiah of Judah who fled to Egypt. The Lord is showing us an important truth. While the exile to Babylon didn't appear to be the best or safest choice, it was better than running to the world when opposition came.

The will of God will not always be the most pleasant to follow, but to follow His will means we will return to the place that has been given to us. In Jesus' day the children of Israel were likened to the fig tree because of this prophecy of Jeremiah. We see an interesting interaction with the fig tree in Matthew 20:18.

Jesus curses the fig tree for not producing fruit at the correct time. Israel had centuries to prepare for the arrival of Messiah, but when He arrived, few who should have recognized Him did so. They were consumed with the letter of the law and were neglecting the spiritual state of those under their authority.

The cursing of the fig tree in relation to the disobedience of the Israelites in Jeremiah and the sin of Adam and Eve in the garden helps us understand the importance of obedience as a fruit of righteousness. In Mark 11 this same miracle is told; it is noted that the tree 'dried up from the roots'. The root of sin, or disobedience to God, has been atoned for by Jesus' sacrifice, and we are now well able to produce the fruits of righteousness through Him.

As believers, we are called to be continually fruitful so that we always have something to share with new believers or those who are not saved. Jesus points out to the bride that this tree is ripening its figs and the vine is blossoming. It is time for her to follow Him and venture out to share the good news.

Have you been tempted to flee what God is calling you to do? What have you found yourself relying on at those times?

Read Matthew 21:19-22

Explain the correlation between the withered fig tree and the mountain. How does faith apply to both?

Read Genesis 3:7

What did Adam and Eve lose after eating the fruit? How did this reveal 'nakedness'?

Revelation 22:2-3

What promises are given concerning fruits in Heaven?

Prayer: Lord, help me follow Your will and direction. I pray that as I follow, the fruit of obedience grows in my heart. Let me be an example of one who follows You, and let Your goodness show in my life. Help me to renew my mind daily so I would know the Word and see the lies of the enemy before I'm deceived. In Jesus' name. Amen.

Activation: Adam and Eve ate a fruit, but it was an act of disobedience. It is possible to produce rotten fruit. These are fruits that develop when we haven't renewed our minds to the Word or we have continued to believe lies of the enemy. Some of the hardest fruits to find are those that seem like the truth but are just a little bit 'off'. This was Satan's temping of Eve, "Has God said?"

We must know the Word to produce good fruit. Today, ask God to show you areas where your fruit could use improvement. In your journal, write down these fruits and what possible lies or partial truths you believe. Beside those lies write down some verses that address God's truth concerning them so that you may renew your mind to the Word and produce good fruit.

Behold Him

[So I went with him, and when we were climbing the rocky steps up the hillside, my beloved shepherd said to me] O my dove, [while you are here] in the seclusion of the clefts in the solid rock, in the sheltered and secret place of the cliff, let me see your face, let me hear your voice; for your voice is sweet, and your face is lovely.

The Song of Songs 2:14

As the children of Israel journeyed from Egypt to the Promised Land, they reached Mount Horeb (Sinai) where Moses received the Ten Commandments and the Torah from God. All throughout the journey, the Israelites witnessed and experienced the miracles of God, but Moses understood there was more to the Father than miraculous experiences. He sought the experience of His person and His glory.

Glory, an often-uttered word inside the church, is the radiance and splendor of the Father, but it is also a heart of reverence, honor, and love. It was God's love and honor of Moses that moved Him to show Himself. Within that place of refuge in the cleft of the rock, Moses experienced the glory of God, the part of Him that resounds throughout creation.

These places of refuge for the bride are found within the secret places of Jesus, and He says turn to me and see how I can transform you. Just as Moses returned from the experience on Sinai with a radiance that was visible to everyone within the camp, we can be transformed by our time with Jesus.

He says this is the place in which we are free to show ourselves as we are. It is here that we show our face and pour out our fervent desires and dreams. These secluded places are found as we follow Him, even up the rocky slopes of mountains we face in life.

Our bridegroom asks for an honor, but it can be difficult to unveil ourselves. Deep within our hearts we know our weaknesses and fears, but it is only with this continual unveiling that we are ever transformed into His image and likeness. Deep within we must be convinced of His gentle love, for perfect love casts out fear.

What is the significance of unveiling ourselves? Have you hidden behind a veil from God? Why?

Read 2 Corinthians 3:18

When we unveil ourselves, what happens?

Read Psalms 71:3

What strong images are used to describe God? Write out the ways you would describe the Father's faithfulness.

Read Exodus 34: 6-11

What does God actively do for believers?

Prayer: God, Thank You that You are love. Help me see past all the good things that flow from You that I would see who You are. Let my heart expand to know all Your goodness, and help me unveil my eyes so I would see clearly. In Jesus' name. Amen.

Activation: God has many names given throughout the Word. Each name encompasses a distinct facet of His being. In your journal, write down the names of God and their meaning and everyday focus on learning more about each one. Watch your faith and trust grow as you learn more about the person of God.

Refine Me

[My heart was touched and I fervently sang to him my desire] Take for us the foxes, the little foxes that spoil the vineyards [of our love], for our vineyards are in blossom.

The Song of Songs 2:15

Once the bride sees the true love of her bridegroom, she feels a touch within her that causes her heart to cry out. This deep desire to express herself and her feelings openly is the outworking of her understanding that despite her imperfections, he sees her as beautiful. However, instead of singing of her joy at His love and affections, she focuses on problems and her inner weakness rather than the strength found in her bridegroom.

One must ask why she focuses on these little foxes so intently? If her beloved asked for her deepest desires to be shown and unveiled before Him, why choose to ask that He catch the little troubles that eat of the fruit? While many new believers focus on the sins of the flesh that are obvious, it's often the little things that we allow to remain in our lives that cause us the greatest agony.

These hidden sins are those that are oftentimes easily overlooked. They are frequently deep within our hearts and minds and are viewed apart from the 'big' sins most Christians are abhorrent to. While no one who professes Jesus as their Lord would view murder or thievery as acceptable, many of those same Christians wouldn't express the same disgust toward gossip, resentment, or doubt. Sin itself is disobedience to the word or command of God. To Adam and Eve, it may have seemed a small thing to eat fruit of a tree, but in the greater orchestra of creation it leads to the fall of man.

Though it is true we are the righteousness of God in Christ, one must never minimize what the Word of God forbids. When we understand that our ability to bear fruit for the kingdom is at stake, we should double our efforts at disposing of these little sins.

Selfishness is a root in many lives today. Self-importance is a justification many use to turn a blind eye to following the Lord where He leads. It justifies our busyness and our habits, but we must remember Jesus tells us the greatest of all is servant of all. To humble ourselves is to overcome selfish desires.

Romans 7:8 "But sin, finding an opportunity through the commandment [to express itself] produced in me every kind of coveting *and* selfish desire. For without the Law sin is dead [the recognition of sin is inactive]."

Doubt. For many it is hard to understand the truth that the spiritual realm is more real than this temporal one. The truth is we are the righteousness of God in Christ Jesus, we are above and not beneath, but we still experience situations and circumstances that are contrary to what is true in the Spirit. It does not mean we have lost our salvation or that God is against us, it means we have allowed the enemy to manipulate our emotions and thoughts into believing something that is not true.

When we view people and circumstance as subject to the ruler of this world, who is Satan, we begin to understand that emotions, thoughts, situations, etc. can be lies and traps of the enemy. Deceptions of the enemy allowed unchecked in our lives produces doubt. It causes many to question the truth of the Word. It causes many to justify unbelief as though God's promises are not equally available.

Matthew 21:21 Jesus replied to them, "I assure you *and* most solemnly say to you, if you have faith [personal trust and confidence in Me] and do not doubt *or* allow yourself to be drawn in two directions, you will not only do what was done to the fig tree, but even if you say to this mountain, 'Be taken up and thrown into the sea,' it will happen [if God wills it]."

Lust. While many believe that lust is the sexual desires of the flesh, we see in 1 John it also includes shameful pursuits and ungodly longing. Any ungodly longing is a lust that our flesh craves whether it be fame, indulgence, or the approval of others. We must understand that the desires of God should be supreme in our lives. It is when we follow His will for our lives that our innermost desires He created within us are fulfilled.

1 John 2:16-17 'For all that is in the world—the lust of the flesh [craving for sensual gratification] and the lust of the eyes [greedy longings of the mind] and the pride of life [assurance in one's own resources or in the stability of earthly things]—these do not come from the Father but are from the world [itself].The world is passing away, and with it its lusts

[the shameful pursuits and ungodly longings]; but the one who does the will of God *and* carries out His purposes lives forever.'

Gossip. If the people of God understood the damage and destruction that came through the tongue, few would ever speak without great thought and care. It is through His words that God formed the universe and we are made in His image. Our words form the world around us and shape our own lives and destinies. The Word tells us that the tongue holds the power of life and death. When we gossip, it is not words we speak over ourselves, but rather words over the lives of others. Do we speak death over others, or life?

Proverbs 16:28 'A perverse man spreads strife, and one who gossips separates intimate friends.'

Murmuring. While gossip is speaking about others, murmuring is showing unbelief in our own lives. Murmuring when we face challenges voices our doubt in God's ability to deliver us. This is an entrance for the devil to wreak havoc in our lives as he is then able to manipulate people and circumstances because of our unbelief. It is good to remember that Satan can't read our minds, but he does hear what we say and he acts accordingly.

Philippians 2:14-15a 'Do everything without murmuring or questioning [the providence of God], 15 so that you may prove yourselves to be blameless *and* guileless, innocent *and* uncontaminated, children of God without blemish in the midst of a [morally] crooked and [spiritually] perverted generation.'

Resentment is a deep-rooted desire of our flesh to have more and to compare ourselves to others. Resentment enters when we see others with the things we desire for ourselves. We make room when we express jealousy or when we claim being wronged. If left unchecked in our lives, jealousy leads us to gossip and harboring hateful hearts and evil thoughts toward others.

Ephesians 4:27 'And do not give the devil an opportunity [to lead you into sin by holding a grudge, or nurturing anger, or harboring resentment, or cultivating bitterness].'

Pride. It's not always easy to see the roots of pride in our lives, but it is necessary we keep vigilant in our searching them out. It was through pride that Lucifer fell from Heaven. Thinking in his heart he could be God and take His throne, he rebelled and was cast out. While we are the righteousness of God in Christ, we must understand that it is only through Him that we are redeemed. To root out this destructive force, we must seek and understand humility.

Proverbs 16:8 "Pride goes before destruction, And a haughty spirit before a fall."

Read 1 John 2:16

What comes from the world? Can you give more examples than are listed in this verse?

Read Romans 7:4-5; Romans 7:25

What changes in our heart in regards to sin when we were born again?

1 Timothy 5:24

Are there different types of sin? How does this verse explain the difference between them? Are they truly different or do they only appear different?

Prayer: Thank you Lord for helping me overcome these little foxes. Let it be my continual desire to honor and glorify Your name in all the earth. In Jesus' name. Amen.

Activation: Hearing from God isn't always the most pleasant. If any of us were to think back to our childhoods, we would recall the occasional rebuke from our parents. It was out of love and the desire we grow as individuals that our parents reprimanded us. There are times God will do the same, but the major difference is we often don't listen to His direction because we don't like it. Write down each of the little foxes listed above in your journal. Over the next week ask God if any of them have taken root in your life. If you hear the nudge of yes, ask Him how it can be pulled from your heart. Tackle the issues with His help, and everything will renew in your life.

Claim His Truth

[She said distinctly] My beloved is mine and I am his! He pastures his flocks among the lilies.

The Song of Songs 2:16

While the heart of this bride is in the right place, she is still viewing her heart's desire as a possession. She cried out 'I am His!', but it is in response to her reception of her beloved's love. Her perception of love is still the feeling of contentment and desire, but the word of God tells us it is far more than feelings and emotions.

The love of the Father is one that not only shows an expression of kindness and goodness, but it also shows a selflessness that transcends what we comprehend. Mere human love often is a desire to love only for what may be gained, but this God-like love is devoted to the hearts and minds of others.

His deep love for every individual moved Him to give a gift to all who would accept. It was to a lost and very broken world that God sent His Son, even knowing that not all would accept His precious gift.

The laying down of one's life for the benefit of others is the greatest example of selfless love. It was in the laying down of His life that Jesus redeemed mankind to fellowship with the Father. It is only by this selfless love that we overcome our own selfish desire to follow Jesus for what He gives us.

Following Jesus to simply reap the benefits of the Christian life will gain one only a shallow relationship with Him. A vast multitude followed Him, but only a few were His disciples, experiencing the depths of relationship with Him. This bride-to-be notes here she is

His! Her identity in Christ is becoming more real to her, and even though she makes mistakes in her immaturity, she is loved by the King.

What is your greatest desire in following the Lord?

Read Luke 6:17

Name the two groups in this verse. What do you think the significance of Jesus coming to a level place is? Where do you think He was previously?

Read 1 John 4:8

Define love in your own words. How do you think God's love differs from your definition?

Read John 3:16

How does God love in this verse? Is this similar to your definition above?

Prayer: Lord, help me keep my eyes focused on who You are. Please show me where I have thought of You as an object or someone to love on my own terms. I praise You for your goodness and mercy which show me the truth in love, and I praise Your name for a relationship that is unshakeable. In Jesus' name. Amen.

Activation: Have you ever seen selfless love in action? Many of us have. Today I challenge you to honor someone who has done something for you or a loved one selflessly. It's never done for praise, but to praise someone is to encourage them. Let yourself be a vessel of honor and praise for another today. Ask God how you can best show your appreciation and let them know God sees and cares for them.

Never Leaving

[Then, longingly addressing her absent shepherd, she cried] Until the day breaks and the shadows flee away, return hastily, O my beloved, and be like a gazelle or a young hart as you cover the mountains [which separate us].

The Song of Songs 2:17

Just as the darkness of winter flees from the bride, she states here the shadows themselves flee away. These traces of her old self that crowd out the presence of her bridegroom must be dealt with so He may have full reign in her heart. She begins to understand that it is not under her own power that she deals with these traces of sin and self. She calls upon her beloved to return to her quickly that the presence of Him would deal with these shadows.

One must wonder how this heart does not perceive her bridegroom. Earlier she noted He was near, just out of view, but here she believes He left her. We must all remember that once we have given our lives over to Christ, He is always with us. He is our Immanuel, God with us, at all times. The Father never defines us by our problems or struggles, and always speaks of who we were made to be in Christ.

Have you experienced a time when it felt God had left you? Explain why you felt He left.

Read Deuteronomy 31:8

How does this verse change your perception of His presence?

Read Romans 6:14

What holds no power over us? What do we have in its place?

Prayer: I thank You and praise You Lord that You never leave me and You never forsake me. Help me to see You everywhere as I go about my day, and especially help me see those who need Your love. Let my life be a vessel for the kingdoms glory. In Jesus' name. Amen.

Activation: Earlier you wrote in your journal how God sees you. I'd like you to do this again today. Ask the Father how He sees you and your progress. Write down all you hear, and compare what you've written to the previous list. How have things changed? Are your words more encouraging? Motivating? Positive?

CHAPTER 3

Seek and Ye Shall Find

A Place of Rest

In the night I dreamed that I sought the one whom I love. [She said] I looked for him but could not find him.

The Song of Solomon 3:1

Early on in our new life with the bridegroom, we are drawn by His loving-kindness and tender ways. As we progress through the pleasant phases of joining ourselves to Him, we begin to experience some of the heat and trials of self-denial. He is a good shepherd and will gently prod us when we must face hindrances in following Him, but earlier He made a call to this betrothed. He called her up the mountain with Him.

While we often face trials concerning the denial of ourselves, we also face trails and obstacles the enemy to our faith would put in front of us. Rather than see the course He called her to, she cried out that the foxes must be dealt with in order for her to follow. Many feel it is impossible to serve God while not perfect, but the Word tells us this is not true. We are well able to serve the King of Kings as we are being transformed into His image. This is the course of service Paul calls us to run (Hebrews 12:1).

Our course in life brings us through many trials that give us a powerful testimony to the glory of our Father. Often after our initial encounter with Jesus, we boldly declare it is our purpose to follow Him wherever He leads. Then as we grow used to His presence in our lives,

His peace and love bring us to a place of comfort few are ready to leave. It is why Paul tells us time and again that we must grow from glory to glory.

This bride ignored the call of her bridegroom. It is why she feels the separation in her place of rest, for she should not be resting. He is calling her attention to deeper issues of the heart. Many times we are oblivious to Christ's working in our lives, and if we yield to His working, we grow stronger and mature from glory to glory. If we fail to yield our hearts to Him, our lives will echo with the distance between us and our Savior. He hasn't removed Himself from us, nor has He rejected us, but rather we feel the separation because He is jealous in His love for us and desires we mature and grow.

Have you encountered the feeling of unworthiness in pursuing the things of God? What made you believe you were unworthy?

Read Philippians 3:13-15
The Apostle Paul had every reason to feel unworthy because of his past. What important lesson can we learn from this verse?

Read 2 Corinthians 3:18
In your own words, describe what you believe glory to glory means. How does it relate to what you just learned?

Read Isaiah 58

The Lord is speaking of fasting and service. What does He say about the prayer and fasting of the people? What does He say about their service? How does this blessing of service apply to you?

Prayer: Lord, I praise You that no matter where I am in my walk with You, I can bring increase to the kingdom. I thank You that I am the righteousness of God in Christ. On this walk of intimacy, I am transformed and live holy sanctified unto You. Help me forget those things which are behind me, and to stay focused on what You have set before me. In Jesus' name. Amen.

Activation: One of the ways we deny ourselves and give our lives to the service of the Lord is through prayer and fasting. Take some time to ask God what you should fast from so that you might pray. What would He ask you to pray about? How long should you fast and pray? Write down what you hear and begin your service to the King.

The Right Direction

So I decided to go out into the city, into the streets and broad ways, and seek him whom my soul loves. I sought him, but I could not find him.

The Song of Solomon 3:2

Surrendering her will, the bride decides to find her bridegroom. However, she doesn't follow the path that brought her to Him before. She decides to try and find Him in a city of men. She decided to obey, but it was on her own terms and in her own way. In the very same way, we will never find the fulfillment of Christ if we do not pursue Him in the way He tells us He is to be found.

When we search the world over for what can satisfy our soul, we are left lacking. To this point, the bride has enjoyed the fruits of knowing her Savior and the redemption through the cross. After knowing the salvation of the cross, she begins to understand His indwelling presence and the joy of relationship with Him. The banner of love and the place of rest are only the beginning of all He is. She was called away from the place of rest to the next glory.

It is amazing this bed of repose was once so comforting. Now it is empty and uncomfortable. She understands it is only due to the presence of her bridegroom that she felt any comfort or peace. However enamored she may feel, her soul isn't matured, and her field of seeking is now the face of everyone she meets. She must realize that He did not leave her, and He is not to be sought in others. It is a mistake many believers make in their progress of betrothal.

How might one search for God in a human way? Have you done this before? Why?

Read Job 23: 8-14

Does Job see the Lord in any of these verses? Where is the Lord?

Read Hebrews 6:1

Growing in Christ is like learning new and progressively more difficult truths. What is the end result of this learning?

Read John 14:21

What is the promise of this verse? What do we do to see the promise in our lives?

Prayer: Thank You Jesus that I have been redeemed from the dead works. I praise Your name that You will never leave me, nor will You ever forsake me. Help me to know You more, and understand Your ever-present help. Let me glorify You and be a written epistle for Your kingdom. In Jesus' name. Amen.

Activation: Psalm 37 is one of my favorite psalms to read during difficult times. Often it's when we lose sight of our Savior that the circumstances and thoughts begin to plague us most. Refocus our attention on Jesus will help soothe our minds and allow joy to rise up no matter what we face. Read Psalm 37 in its entirety. Write down all this psalm asks of us, then go back and write down all God promises to do. Meditate on the significance of this over the next week.

Spiritual Guidance

The watchmen who go about the city found me, to whom I said, "Have you seen him whom my soul loves?"

The Song of Solomon 3:3

The surest rest is one in which we have no worries or anxieties. It is why the watchmen of the city were so vital to its function. They kept vigil day and night watching for messengers, tradesmen, and enemies. The watchmen look into the darkness and alert the inhabitants of what evil is coming. One must ask then why they have found this bride to be wandering the city.

The only power the enemy holds over our lives as believers is the power we willingly or unknowingly give him. It is why God in His wisdom set authority in place (Hebrews 13:17).

Elders of the church who understand the need for discipleship help guide believers along on their spiritual path. It is an authority that teaches the Word, ministers the Word, and prays the Word over us, and is the flow of life from the head, which is Christ.

Certainly, the watchmen in this bride's life noticed her errant wanderings. Accountability in the lives of believers will help us develop deeper relationships with others and with Jesus. This accountability with others, who are also on a path of deepening relationship with the bridegroom, allows us to share our hearts in a meaningful and personal way. The act of heartfelt sharing of triumphs and struggles on our path bind our hearts with others and it allows us to learn from each other and depend upon one another for prayer and guidance. Though we do not see the answer they give her concerning her search, we do see the result of her encounter with these vigilant watchers.

Have you ever received correction from another believer? How did you respond to the correction?

Read Hebrews 10:24-25
How do correction and encouragement differ? In what ways are they similar? What is a major way we can encourage one another according to Paul?

Read Ephesians 4:15
How might one correct the belief or behavior of another in love? Why is love so necessary in correction?

Read Hebrews 13:17

Why is it important to remember this verse when receiving correction? What spiritual authorities do you have in your life who may correct you?

Read Isaiah 62:6 and Ezekiel 33:2-7

What is the role of a watchman? How do they watch over the body of Christ?

Prayer: Thank You Lord for all the people in my life who help me in my walk with You. Let my heart be humble so that I would receive correction with the correct attitude, and let my mind be ready to understand the truth that is being spoken in love. I pray now for wisdom and revelation of Your Word for strength and help. In Jesus' name. Amen.

Activation: We often need help from other believers to reorient our lives toward Christ, but we can also be the ones used by God to point others to Him. Ask the Lord today how you can be used to help point others to Him.

Grace upon Grace

I had gone but a little way past them when I found him whom my soul loves. I held him and would not let him go until I had brought him into my mother's house, and into the chamber of her who conceived me.

The Song of Solomon 3:4

After her encounter with the spiritual authorities in her life, the bride soon finds the object of her search, as it was 'but a little way past them'. Note they did not approach the bridegroom for her, but they did share with her where He may be found. As we shed the old man and put on the new one, we find over time that the process of maturing, learning, and deepening our faith brings to the front new issues that must be addressed.

On many occasions, these blind spots or points of weakness are easy for others to see, and if we have opened ourselves to the input of others through accountability, they are able to, in love, bring attention to those areas. It is our process of sanctification that points out our misplaced desires, and when addressed, quickly leads us past the point of weakness to newness with our bridegroom.

It is a joyous reunion with her love after a period of separation. Such is her joy that she clings to Him with fervor. She declares that she will bring Him to her mother's house. Remember those mountains her bridegroom wished her to climb? What greater mountain to face than the one of familiarity.

The most difficult places to bring our Lord are the familiar spaces of family, work, and friends. Rejection and ridicule may follow from the mouths and actions of those we held in regard. What would we do with our bridegroom should those whose opinions matter; reject Him? No, we would never reject the One who brought us to this place where we lay aside all things. In fact, the bride clings to Him as though if she hangs on to Him tightly enough, she would never experience His absence again.

One must notice that it is the bride-to-be that is pulling the bridegroom to her mother's chamber. In Chapter 1 verse 4 she exclaimed 'Draw Me!' rejoicing that He had brought her in His chambers. Why then is she so vehement on bringing her love into the chambers of the one who conceived her?

Previously He brought the bride into His chamber where He revealed the intimacy of love and grace through salvation. Now the bride in her fervor to offer something to the bridegroom pulls Him into her innermost chamber. She is beginning to understand that life with Christ is more than experience and His presence. He is far more than one who makes us happy or brings us peace. Allowing Him freedom to enter and change our inner personality will bring us closer to Him and closer to discipleship.

While the watchman can't bring the bride to the bridegroom, they can point the way. Have you ever experienced someone helping or pointing you to Jesus? How did they encourage you to find Him?

Read John 14:2

It was Hebrew custom for the bridegroom to add a room onto his Father's house for his bride. How does this verse encourage you in pursuing your bridegroom?

Read Proverbs 27:17

In your own words, describe what 'iron sharpening iron' means.

Read Hebrews 12:7-8

How does God view us? Why is this significant? Does it change how you view chastisement?

Prayer: Lord, thank You that whenever I call upon Your name for help, You are there. Help me to always embrace you with joy and help me keep my priorities in line with Your Word. Search me Lord and show me Your heart. In Jesus' name. Amen.

Activation: Read Ephesians 3:16 in the Amplified Bible. Take time today to write the meaning of this verse in your own words. How does the understanding of it change your perspective of Christ in you?

Part 2: A Deeper Love The Song of Solomon 3:5-7:1

Transfiguration of Love

I adjure you, O daughters of Jerusalem, by the gazelles or by the hinds of the field that
you stir not up nor awaken love until it pleases.

The Song of Solomon 3:5

While it's difficult to lose sight of the object of our affections, it is far more exhausting to work through the trials of life without our bridegroom Jesus. The bridegroom is speaking to the daughters again and states He adjures them. To adjure means to completely and solemnly swear something by repeating a declaration or oath seven times. The repetition of the oath seven times signifies it is complete and that the one swearing would never dare to break the promise.

The temple priests adjured when they conducted the sin offering for the people. The priest would sacrifice the bull as an offering for unintentional or unknown sins of the people, and the blood would be shaken in front of the veil of the sanctuary seven times. The request of this oath from the daughters signifies an important understanding of the influence others have in our lives.

To not stir up love is to allow others to learn at their own pace. It's not necessary that we prod others along the path of intimacy or discipleship with Christ. A wholly righteous pursuit of Him is borne out of our hearts. Though these daughters would try to stir up something within her, He told them she is in a divine rest in His embrace. He reminds them of this cleansing within her heart, and that only He can stir her from this place of rest.

Have you ever been pushed toward God by friends, family, or your spouse? What was the result of this push to seek God? Was your heart ready?

Read Romans 8:18

What glory do you think will be revealed? How do you believe this will be revealed in you?

Read Hebrews 9:11-12

Redemption is eternal and accomplished once and for all. How do these verses encourage you to seek Him fully today?

Read Hosea 2:14-20

What promises are given to those betrothed to the Lord? What does He ask of us?

Prayer: Lord, help me respect the faith walk of others. Let me keep focused on Your work in me and encourage others without stirring them up to unhealthy pursuits. I thank You for grace and mercy now. In Jesus' name. Amen.

Application: We've talked a lot about forgiving others, but today we will focus on forgiving ourselves. Many times we feel the guilt of 'shoulda, woulda, coulda' in our Christian lives. We may have felt the push toward God from others and feel guilty we didn't pursue Him. It's possible you've experienced hard times and been angry with God or other people.

Whatever your circumstances may be, respecting the faith walk of others means we also respect our own.

In your journal write down some of the things you've felt guilt over. Make a point to forgive yourself for those things, and take time this week to speak with God about all of them. Did He give you a different perspective of that situation? Understand He knew the end from the beginning and will use all things for good.

A Life Changed

Who or what is this [she asked] that comes gliding out of the wilderness like stately pillars of smoke perfumed with myrrh, frankincense, and all the fragrant powders of the merchant?

The Song of Solomon 3:6

Only by the power of the Lord Jesus could we glide from the wilderness. The temptations of Satan are no match for the King of Kings and Lord of Lords, and through His victory we are made victorious. He came as a humble servant to redeem mankind for the glory of the Father, and when He triumphed in the wilderness it was by the Word and through the Word.

It's time for the bride to leave the wilderness of wandering for a place of provision and rest. The steps of growth as we grow into Christ and walk away from Egypt are gradual and measured. The children of Israel didn't need to spend forty years wandering through the wilderness, and neither do believers. The children of Israel are called our natural examples of spiritual truths, and we can learn much from their wanderings and failings in the wilderness.

The heady fragrance of myrrh again reaches the senses of the bride. While before she held this thorny bundle close to her heart, she now perceives deeper things. Myrrh, or מרר marar, as the Hebrews called it, comes from the root which means 'bitterness'. In the hours before His arrest, Jesus fervently prayed in the Garden of Gethsemane. With the weight of the cross before Him and the burden of the world's sin, He sweat great drops of blood.

This bitter suffering of our Lord is much like the bitter, yet aromatic, tears of myrrh. When pierced, the branches of the plant weep red drops which harden and are tenderly gathered. We are to share in our Lord's sufferings. It is not to bear the burden of sin, but rather we are to share the bitter burden of laying aside our lives just as Christ did when He came to this earth. It is at His side that we lay down our lives in obedience.

The properties of myrrh give us a deeper understanding of our Lord and King. It was a main component in the embalming spice and kept things from rotting. Because of this, it was used on the linen wraps of the dead. Its use was first prescribed by God to Moses as the main component of the anointing oil for Aaron as high priest. The other component of this oil was frankincense.

Frankincense, or לבונה lebonah, means white or pure. It is grown in the high mountains of Lebanon within the snowy reaches. The milky white resin of the tree was gathered in a similar fashion to myrrh, though in the case of frankincense, this resin never hardens. This aromatic resin was the main spice burned upon the altar of incense, which continually burned in the temple. It was this incense that carried the prayers of the saints to the Father.

Jesus lived a life of prayer upon the earth. After His ascension, we are told He is always making intercession for us before the Father (Hebrews 7:25). We too are called to live a life perfumed with prayer. To be perfumed with prayer, one must absorb its fragrance and spread it through practice. By doing so, our lives become pillars and foundations of faith that help support the spread of this Good News of salvation.

Have you viewed your prayer life as an essential part of your faith walk? Explain.

Read John 6:32

What is the significance of Jesus being the bread from Heaven? How does this bread differ from the manna given to the Israelites in the wilderness?

Read Luke 4:13

What happened when Jesus overcame the temptation in the wilderness?

Read Revelation 5:8

In light of this verse, how important are your prayers? Who hears them?

Read Joel 2:28-32

What promises are given in these verses? When will we see pillars of smoke?

Prayer: Thank you Lord for providing for all my needs. I pray that the Word would take greater root in my heart and that You would reveal to me the necessity of prayer. I thank You that You provide bread for my spirit and soul daily. In Jesus' name. Amen.

Activation: Many of us have only vague understandings of what prayer looks like. We often think of folded hands and bowed heads, but in the Word, we see prayer takes on many forms. Prayer in its simplest form is communication with God. It can be questions, conversations, requests, worship, silent, or any other way He chooses to speak. Today, try communicating with the Father in your quiet place in a new way. It may seem awkward at first, but that's only because it's new. Then throughout your day, try and communicate with Him on a regular basis. This is what Paul mentions in 1 Thessalonians 5:17 when he speaks of praying without ceasing.

The Mercy Seat

Behold, it is the traveling litter (the bridal couch) of Solomon. Sixty mighty men are around it, of the mighty men of Israel.

The Song of Solomon 3:7

The King enters the scene upon His bridal couch, and the joyous time of celebration is set to begin. This couch is not only a place of rest, but a place of honor and respect. It is surrounded by the sixty mighty men of Israel who guard and keep the king upon his seat. This mention of sixty mighty men surrounding the couch brings an interesting correlation to the tabernacle.

In Exodus 20 we read the account of the construction of the tabernacle in the wilderness. The tabernacle in the wilderness was built to certain specifications which the Lord gave Moses. The outer wall of the tabernacle was adorned in great sheets of linen, which were supported by sixty pillars. Each of the pillars were made of acacia wood and covered in gold. Acacia wood was considered the highest quality as the grain prevented penetration by insects or other 'corrupting' agents, and they were then overlain with gold.

The only way to enter the tabernacle was through the eastern gate, which was covered with a tightly woven piece of linen made of scarlet, blue, and purple, a reminder that heaven's throne would provide sacrifice for man. Once one entered the tabernacle, it was possible to find forgiveness from sin and be restored to fellowship with God.

When one would enter through the gate, their first sight would be the brazen altar. It was a reminder that man had a sinful nature due to Adam and Eve's disobedience. It was formed from acacia wood and overlaid in bronze, symbolic of the judgement of sin. While these sacrifices covered sin, they must be performed year after year. Standing before the altar of sacrifice, one would know that many more obstacles stood between one and the holy of holies.

One must be washed by the Word to enter the holy of holies; this was symbolized by the bronze laver. Our salvation is our entrance through Christ, but as we mature and progress through to the presence of God we must lay aside our old man and embrace newness in Him.

We are told to wash ourselves with the Word so that we may be presented to Him holy and blameless (Eph 5:25, Heb 10:22).

Beyond the bronze laver lay the inner holy sanctuary. It was covered with linen and goats hair to shield it from the sun and rain. To enter the inner sanctuary, one must be a priest. Inside the inner sanctuary one would find the golden lamp stand, or menorah. It was the only source of light within the enclosure. As it is in our own lives, only through the Word and Holy Spirit do we experience any light from the Father. Growing in relationship with Him, we then carry the light of Jesus to the world around us.

God so desires our fellowship that He sent the bread of heaven, Jesus, as atonement for our sins. Upon the cross our manna from heaven was broken and He cried out 'It is finished!' Within the enclosure before the veil that covered the Ark of the Covenant, one would find the table of showbread. It was also called the bread of the presence as we are always to be in communion with the Father, and each loaf represented a tribe of Israel. Once a week the priests would bake twelve new loaves of bread and coat them in frankincense to replace what they partook of on the Sabbath.

The prayers and intersessions of the saints are sweet fragrances to the Lord. The burning of incense upon the golden altar of incense before the veil was a reminder to all that an intermediary was necessary before the holiness of God. The tabernacle was symbolic of a people separated from the Father by sin, but living in hope of redemption would change all of humanity.

How it must have hurt the heart of the Father to be separated from His children by sin, but He sent His Son to redeem us. Now the curtain is torn and all may enter the presence of God. How joyous must this bride to be find herself when she sees the obstacles between her and her Lord upon the seat have been removed. It is the Lord she sees directly from the gate. No coverings of linen or goats hair will keep her from the sight of her Lord, nor will the sacrifices and repeated washings be necessary to enjoy His company.

Have you felt obstacles separated you from God? Since Jesus has removed these obstacles that keep us from approaching Him, where do you believe the obstacles may come from?

Read Hebrews 10:19

Where are we now able to go? With what attitude can we enter?

Read 1 Corinthians 6:19

How is our body like the tabernacle in the wilderness? What is significant about this?

Read John 10:9 and Exodus 27:16

Jesus is the door or gate by which we enter into salvation. Explain the details and significance of the gate of the tabernacle.

Prayer: I praise You Jesus that all the obstacles are removed and I may approach the throne of grace boldly. I pray that You would help me understand I am now Your tabernacle. Help me keep myself wholly dedicated to You. In Jesus' name. Amen.

Application: "To them God chose to make known how great among the Gentiles are the riches of the glory of this mystery, which is Christ in you, the hope of glory." Col 1:27 ESV Take time today to meditate on this verse. In your journal, write down what you believe this means to have Christ in you the hope of glory. Ask the Father how this should change your actions towards yourself and other believers if Jesus is with you always.

Pillars of Righteousness

They all handle the sword and are expert in war; every man has his sword upon his thigh, that fear be not excited in the night.

The Song of Solomon 3:8

These mighty men surrounding the couch of the king are all warriors. They are the chosen men in the army of the king, and all know and understand the armor and weapons they carry. David's mighty men were not only men of valor, but they were also men of faith who served their king out of love and respect.

These men were lauded in stories for overcoming odds and situations where most would have cowered in fear. Their loyalty to their king shows us a deeper appreciation for the role of king and the importance of our King of love.

During the time of the Philistine's control of Bethlehem, David desired a drink from the well. Three of his mighty men took it upon themselves to fight their way through the line and gather a jug for the king. Upon their return however, David poured the water out on the ground. It was not a rejection of their efforts or willingness to sacrifice themselves for their king, but rather it was an acknowledgement of their love and honor toward him.

It is also a symbolic representation of the pouring of water from the source of Bethlehem. Jesus who is our water of life was poured out for us, and His source was the line of David from the town of Bethlehem. Their desire to please the king and fight for the water in that place is a lesson to all that the journey to the source of life may be challenging, but to draw life from the source of life is our purpose. It is also our call as God's ambassadors on this earth to bring others to this water of life.

We are called to lay aside our own lives and live for our king. These mighty men accompanying the coach of Solomon are warriors just as the body of Christ is to be. We are to be warriors ready to wield the Sword of the Spirit, which is the Word of God, and array ourselves with the full armor made available to us. The armor of God is for our defense while the sword is for attack.

When we realize the truth of our authority in Christ, it almost certainly ensures negative thoughts or circumstances follow. The devil works in many ways to deceive believers, most often with thoughts contrary to the word of God. In order to stand firm in our faith (our ground), Paul tells us to first buckle ourselves with the truth (Eph 6:14).

Just as a Roman soldier would wear his armor daily, we too must daily take up our spiritual weapons and defenses in order to stand firm and overcome. Every Roman solider wore a wide belt about his waist to hold all his pieces of equipment. There were loops for daggers, swords, and ration packs.

These belts were often tied in several places so they never shifted, and would remain in place even if cut during battle. The belt also carried insignias indicating rank, specialty, and identity of its wearer. When the army conquered a city, they would empty their sacks and fill them with treasures.

Paul is telling us something intrinsic to our Christianity in these verses. We must first be secure and solid in the truth of God's Word. Tie it to yourself in many ways, reading it, speaking it, confessing it, praying it. Apply it daily. In the truth of God's Word, all our weapons will hang. They must be in place and ready to use at a moment's notice.

It's also very important to know how to wear the belt. If it is skewed by improper ties, the sword could harm its bearer while being drawn, and it would make the soldier ineffectual against a surprise attack. These improper ties can be anything that hinders our understanding of the Word- religious mindsets, past failures, questions about His will and plan for our lives. Improper ties can be eliminated when we understand who we truly are in Christ. This means having clarity of sound doctrine.

What do you believe? Are you aware of what Christ has done for you? Does the mental knowledge of Christ's victory on the cross translate into your daily life? The truth will set you free. Freedom is free domain for the Holy Spirit to work effectually in and through us.

Our identity in Christ not only strengthens us but also guides us. When we understand our right-standing with God through Jesus, the lies the enemy brings will be easily overcome because we are built on the truth of our identity. When we overcome and see victory in areas of our lives, we see the treasures.

The rich treasury of His glory is boundless. It holds answers to prayers past, present, and future. It holds supernatural treasures of peace, joy, love, righteousness, and healing, all the things riches of this world could never buy. The word encourages all of us to apply the truth daily. Let us all come before Him to daily read, pray, and speak the Word over our lives and families, and we will see the Lord move on our behalf.

Have you taken the time to apply the armor of God? What benefits might one experience if they did this daily?

Read Titus 1:7

Describe the character traits of one who serves the Lord. Does this describe you? Why or why not?

Read Ephesians 6:10-25

What are the pieces of armor and weaponry made available to believers? How would you use this and apply it daily?

Read James 1:2

How might one count hard experiences joyful?

Prayer: Lord, help me understand the authority I have in the name of Jesus. I ask you would remind me to apply the armor of God daily and take up the shield of faith with boldness. Remind me of the Word so I may use the sword of the spirit against the plans and attacks of the enemy. In Jesus' name. Amen.

Application: The Sword of the Spirit, which is the Word of God, is how we fight back against the enemy. Using the example of Jesus in the wilderness, we see that to effectively combat the enemy and emerge victorious, we must have the Word in our mouths. Take time today to search out scriptures that deal with problems you're facing. By having these verses in mind, it is easier to effectively shut down the enemy's attacks against you.

Bearers of the King

King Solomon made himself a palanquin from the [cedar] wood of Lebanon.

The Song of Solomon 3:9

The cedars of Lebanon grew tall and strong, just as our bridegroom desires us to grow. When we are planted by His side, we draw all the necessary nourishment to grow in this manner. The land of Lebanon where the cedars grow is also mountainous and often covered in white. The bridegroom is saying to her again, 'Be strong, be by My side, and be pure."

In Leviticus 14, we read of the offerings made for purification, all of which use cedar wood. The natural oils found within the cedars prevented rot and decay. This wood offering, made along with a live and sacrificed turtle dove, signify our cleansing of guilt. Note that the offering is made after one has been declared clean. We may rest in this completed work.

The king is seated upon a palanquin. In the days of Solomon, it was a mode of transport for the king and other wealthy individuals. They could recline as they were transported upon the shoulders of men. It is similar in many ways to the Ark which was carried by the Levites. The Ark contained the mercy seat, which Jesus now sits upon in Heaven. As believers, we are called to carry Jesus to the world. We do so with the same honor and reverence the Israelite priests carried the mercy seat.

In what ways can we carry Jesus? What way do you carry Him most often?

Read Psalm 104:16

Who planted the cedars of Lebanon? What does this imply the trees are signifying?

Read Isaiah 53:5

What did Jesus suffer? What did these sufferings pay for?

Prayer: Jesus, I thank You that I am purified and sanctified by the Word. Let my mouth speak of Your goodness and grace to others, and let my testimony be one that glorifies Your name. I ask that You would continue to work in my heart and draw me nearer to You. In Jesus' name. Amen.

Activation: Today, ask the Lord how you can continue to carry Him in your daily life. Ask for new ways to reach people with His love.

The Kings Design

He made its posts of silver, its back of gold, its seat of purple, the inside of it lovingly and intricately wrought in needlework by the daughters of Jerusalem.

The Song of Solomon 3:10

The palanquin designed by the king is supported by silver pillars. Throughout the Old Testament, the varying uses of metals was often symbolic of a deeper spiritual meaning. The common thread with the metal silver is one of Redemption.

Our bridegroom paid this price for His bride The Church. His life was to lay aside deity and take on the sinless life in order that we would be redeemed by His blood. The price paid to Judas for his Master was not one for the life of an adult man, but it was the price for an adult female, a woman who was of marrying age, a bride (Leviticus 27:4). The pillars of Christ are now the church at work in the earth. It is through the disciples of Christ that people are brought into relationship and saving knowledge of Him.

Supporting the church and at the very center is He who sent His son for us. The gold back that supports the pillars is its true foundation and the basis for its existence. Unlike silver, gold is not subject to oxidation and corrosion. It is malleable and soft whereas silver is brittle and easily breakable. It is why God instructed the Israelites to overlay all the wood of the tabernacle in gold. It is an earthly type of His incorruptible nature and His divine love.

This purple seat is the seat of a royal priest, and the dye to make it was extracted from a very specific type of shellfish found within the Mediterranean region. The scarcity of the dye made it costly to use and was associated with the priests. The color did not easily fade and would actually brighten under the sun. It is under the Son that we, as the bride of Christ, have been redeemed and given power and authority to use His name on the earth.

Our union with Christ is an ever-growing knowledge and experience of His grace, kindness, compassion and love. This union is available to all who have called upon His name for salvation. As we move closer to Him to experience the intimate nature of this 'marriage', our purpose as the bride becomes clearer.

How would you describe an intimate relationship? How should this apply to our relationship with Christ?

Read Revelation 3:18

What does this gold represent? How would you 'buy' it?

Read Revelation 1:6

What are all believers a part of? What are we called in this verse?

Read Ephesians 4:15-16

Explain how the interior person changes when they join to Christ.

Read Isaiah 62

To whom is this chapter addressed? What promises are given to them?

Prayer: I praise you Lord for changing my heart and making it new. I ask that you would continue to work in my heart and help me see your love for the world. Jesus, help me know you more and show me how to live this life for your glory. In Jesus' name. Amen.

Activation: Take some time to look up the properties of silver and gold. Write down all the things you learn about each precious metal and how this applies to their use in the Bible. You'll be amazed by the interesting things you learn about our God's design.

His Countenance

Go forth, O you daughters of Zion, and gaze upon King Solomon wearing the crown with which his mother [Bathsheba] crowned him on the day of his wedding, on the day of his gladness of heart.

The Song of Solomon 3:11

What a change in tone! No longer does the bridegroom address the daughters of Jerusalem who had been judged. He now addresses them as daughters of Zion, daughters of an incorruptible city with a heavenly king. Once we move past the veil of redemption, we move to the seat, or center, of who He is. God from the beginning shows us this type of marriage as an example of the intimacy He desires with us.

Gaze upon the king! Just as we need to allow the heavens to gaze upon us to solidify within us that we are desired by heaven, so should we gaze upon the source of our salvation. This gaze helps us move forward toward the revelation of Jesus the Bridegroom. It was love upon the cross, but it was also joy.

The joy of the cross was its redemption of individuals. Each member of the body of Christ, each betrothed, was joy to the author and finisher of our faith. This crown placed upon his head was placed there by his mother, but Jesus tells us those who are his disciples are His mother (Matthew 3:35).

A crown is a symbol of Lordship or authority. Here we see it is a crown of joy. It is pleasing to the king when the bride of Christ submits to His Lordship and experiences the fullness of joy found in Him. It is under His authority that we are able to do all things and by His authority that we are made conquerors in this life. Knowing we are already victorious brings joy in times of trouble.

How do you gaze upon the source of salvation? Can you think of any ways you might do this on a daily basis?

Read Hebrews 12:2

What does this verse tell us about Jesus? What does it say about the cross?

Read Luke 8:21

What do you think this verse means for believers?

Prayer: Thank You Lord that as I focus my eyes on You and Your Word, I am changed. I pray for grace and mercy as I grow in You, and that joy is overflowing in my heart. Jesus, help me know you more and be a devout disciple. In Jesus' name. Amen.

Activation: Write down your thoughts on the differences between daughters of Jerusalem and Daughters of Zion. What might this change in address mean? How does the change affect you personally?

CHAPTER 4

Discovering a Deeper Love

Find the Gold

How fair you are, my love [he said], how very fair! Your eyes behind your veil [remind me] of those of a dove; your hair [makes me think of the black, wavy fleece] of a flock of [the Arabian] goats which one sees trailing down Mount Gilead [beyond the Jordan on the frontiers of the desert].

The Song of Solomon 4:1

It is the gentle way of our bridegroom that He always calls out our virtues and strengths rather than our weakness and failures. There are seven total objects referred to in this verse alone. Seven is significant in the Hebrew as it denotes completeness and wholeness.

Again, the eyes of the betrothed look to Him and only Him. These dove eyes are the eyes of spiritual insight in a believer's life. To discern spiritual truth, we must look beyond what we see naturally or what the world would like us to see. Her eyes are hidden behind a veil; there will be times when spiritual insight is to be kept for prayer.

The significance of hair to women of this time was not lost on the bridegroom. In Numbers chapter 6, we see the Nazarene vow which separated a man or woman from the world and unto the Father. This vow was one of the only ways in which an individual could serve the Lord outside the lineage of Aaron. This vow could be for a lifetime or for a designated time of special service.

It is no surprise then that the tabernacle in the desert was covered with the goats' hair offering. The Lord is calling this betrothed to see the importance of her service to the Father. Her vow unto Him set her apart from the others. It is within the sheltered covering of her vow unto the Lord that she finds the holy tabernacle she is to become. It is His dwelling place, holy and set apart.

The vow had many layers of meaning. It allowed one from outside the appointed line of priests to become servants of the Lord, 'grafted' into the tabernacle service, just as the body of Christ is grafted into the root of Abraham. It was a separation from the corruption of death to an incorruptible one in the resurrection of Christ.

As believers, we serve the Father as we are no longer our own. Our Savior made the vow that set apart His life for service, and in His death and resurrection we are free from the taint of sin and the death it brings. It is why the myrrh and frankincense of His anointing have been so vital before now. We have been anointed by His death to serve in this life.

Mount Gilead beyond the Jordan is located within the territory of 3 tribes. Half the mountain belongs to the children of Manasseh. The other half was given to the Reubenites and the Gadites. Gilead was known for its healing balm, but an even more interesting correlation is found in the sons of Jacob.

Gad was the seventh son of Jacob, and the first child by Leah's maid Zylpath. The name given the child conveys an interesting meaning. דד *gadad* means to cut something deep so a valuable thing may be exposed. This deep troubling effort for fortune expresses the deep distress of Leah. How vexing this birth must have been for her. Already given over to sadness at being an undesired or unwanted wife, for this child given through a servant must have exposed deep feelings of grief.

By contrast, Reuben was the first son of Leah and Jacob. His arrival was joyous for both his Father and mother. What a difference between births! His name means to look or take intent notice of something, but the word is often used when the Lord or an angel appears and is noticed by someone.

The tribe of Manasseh, eldest son of Joseph, held the northern section of the mountain of Gilead. The name Manasseh holds many interesting meanings. It is a name with three roots which together form a picture of our bridegroom. The first root meaning to bear or carry a load, the second to lend on interest by means of deception, and the last to forgive and forget by taking away.

When we combine the meanings of each of these names and tribes, we find an expression of love from the Father. This is what the bridegroom is pointing out to the bride.

Look! Take notice of the deep troubling cuts to find value by bearing and carrying the load of forgiving and forgetting the debt accrued through deception.

This is our Mount Gilead, our healing balm, and we are the partakers of its flow in us and through us as His temple.

How do you believe spiritual enlightenment might come? Is this something you currently practice? Why or why not?

Read Ephesians 1:17-19

Once the eyes of our understanding are 'enlightened', what do we understand?

Read 2 Corinthians 4:4

Who spiritually blinded mankind? What was the result of this blindness?

Read Hebrews 5:12-14

According to this verse, how does a person gain discernment?

Prayer: Today's prayer will be from the book of Ephesians. Paul expresses his desire to the church at Ephesus and all believers in chapter 1. Pray Ephesians 1:16-21 out loud.

Activation: After praying this prayer for wisdom, ask the Father if there is something specific He wishes to share with you or show you. Write down what you hear or see from Him.

Meat of the Word

Your teeth are like a flock of shorn ewes which have come up from the washing, of which all are in pairs, and none is missing among them.

The Song of Solomon 4:2

Moving to new heights with His bride, the bridegroom praises her in a new way. He praises her vow to serve Him and make her body His tabernacle. To understand the importance of teeth and freshly shorn ewes, we must look at the roots of these words.

The Hebrew word *shanan* is where we get the word *shen* for tooth. *Shanan* means to sharpen, especially the mind. To gain knowledge, it is said one must 'chew' on information in order that it be processed and understood. We all partake of milk until we have matured enough to chew solid foods. In the same manner, Paul encourages us in 1 Corinthians chapter 3 to grow and mature in our understanding of the Word and the power of Christ in us.

The shearing of sheep takes place in springtime. This 'new season' in Him begins with the shedding of our old man and taking on the new life. The wool was most often used in garments, but not in the garments of the priests. We read in Ezekiel 44 the woolen garments caused sweat which was not permitted within the temple. The sweat of our brow was part of the curse laid upon Adam and Eve for their sin in the garden, and we have been redeemed from this curse of toil by our bridegroom.

These freshly shorn ewes that have been washed of the filth and dirt of this world and are again made white and pure. Just as they have been cleansed, we too must cleanse our minds of worldly ideas and begin to chew on the solid food of the word. It is promised that as we feast on the solid food of the Word, that we bear fruit in our lives. This fruitfulness is the glory of the Father and the sign of His disciples (John 15:8).

Fruitfulness in the spirit is dependent on our reception of the Spirit. It's why the brides' teeth are noted in pairs and none are missing. One must never pick and choose what to believe from the Word of God. If we believe God has sent His son for salvation, one must also believe we are more than conquerors through Him. If we pick and choose what we believe from the Word, we have in our minds created a God intellectually acceptable to serve and that is not one that exists.

How does one 'chew' on the Word? How often do you feel it's necessary to do this?

Read Ephesians 5:26

How does the Word act like water to wash us?

Read Hebrews 5:12-14

Describe what the 'milk' of the Word would be. Describe what the 'meat' of the Word might be.

Read John 4:34

What is 'meat' to Jesus? What is the meat of the Word for you?

Prayer: Lord, I praise you for revealing to me the deep things of the Word. I pray my heart and mind are ready for even more wisdom and understanding from You. Let me be an example of a wise and tempered believer, and let my life bring Your name glory. In Jesus' name. Amen.

Activation: Today, ask the Holy Spirit to reveal to you an area of the Word you have had difficulty believing. Perhaps you've felt like you aren't a worthy mouthpiece of the Lord. Write down what area was revealed to you, and make a point to read and study all that the Word says is truth. Be ready to activate this in your life!

Beauty in Balance

Your lips are like a thread of scarlet, and your mouth is lovely. Your cheeks are like halves of a pomegranate behind your veil.

The Song of Solomon 4:3

Lips that speak the truth of our king's sacrifice are prized beyond measure. The bridegroom is praising the mouth of this bride as a witness for her Lord. When we speak in agreement with the Holy Spirit, the abundance of the Father permeates our lives. The pomegranate behind the veil is this abundance. Within the pomegranate are many seeds. The truth of these seeds within our hearts and minds flow out our mouths and are planted in the hearts of those around us.

We should desire to be so full of love for our bridegroom that out of the abundance of His love and sacrifice in our hearts we speak a thread of scarlet among the people. To share the heart of our king we must see the world as He sees the world. It is at this point in our lives we turn our hearts from all that our king gives us to what we now have to give others.

Read Joshua 2:21, Matthew 27:28

What did this thread of scarlet represent?

Read Psalm 12:6

What are words spoken by a believer to be like?

Read Luke 6:45

How do we know when God's Word has taken root in our hearts?

Read Luke 8:11

What are the seeds and truths we speak?

Read 2 Corinthians 9:10

Who provides this seed to sow, and what are the consequences of sowing it?

Prayer: Lord, let my lips give You praise forever and let my words be sweet to those who hear them. Let my mouth share nothing but what I hear from the Father. I praise You for Your goodness and mercy that have made my full of joy and hope. In Jesus' name. Amen.

Activation: The truest words to speak and share with the hurting and needy are the words of our Lord. Make an effort this week to memorize verses of scripture that are uplifting and hope filled. The book of Proverbs is an excellent place to begin. Write down the verses you memorize in your journal.

A Strong Tower

Your neck is like the tower of David, built for an arsenal, whereon hang a thousand bucklers, all of them shields of warriors.

The Song of Solomon 4:4

Before her neck was tied and bound with baubles of the world, He now sees it as a pillar of strength and defense. It is a strength that encompasses her without making her stiff-necked or stubborn. This tower of David, built by a man who was after God's own heart, was at the heart of the king's home.

This tower holds the arsenal of the king. Our Lord defeated the enemy, and by His victory we are overcomers. The weapons of our warfare are stored within us. As we seek His face, the words of our testimony give praise and glory to the one who delivered us.

When words of the heart come forth, they pass through the vocal chords and are spoken from the mouth. To guard one's mouth while renewing the mind, we must understand that these words must pass the test whether or not they are God's words or the enemy's words, God's will or our will. All spiritual warfare is fought for the souls and wills of men.

Have you experienced spiritual warfare? What was under attack? How did you overcome the attack?

Psalm 62:2

Who has built this strong tower? Why is the builder important?

Read Ephesians 6:16

What does this shield represent? How does this shield keep believers safe?

1 Chronicles 12:8

Describe the mighty men of David.

Prayer: Thank you Jesus for giving me strength. I pray that You would help me keep focused on the authority I have in Your name to overcome the enemy and remain victorious. In Jesus' name. Amen.

Activation: One of the greatest benefits of memorizing scripture is having truth ready to be spoken. When Jesus was tempted, He spoke the Word of God in response to temptation. Think of one area of your life where you are feeling tempted or attacked by the enemy. Look up verses of scripture that share the truth to counter the enemy's lies. Add those verses to your list to memorize and use them when Satan accuses you.

A Heart of Righteousness

Your two breasts are like two fawns, like twins of a gazelle that feed among the lilies.

The Song of Solomon 4:5

The bridegroom has noted seven distinct features of the bride, and each feature holds a key to the complete nature of individuals who are followers of Christ. He speaks lastly of the attribute most vital to our discipleship, our hearts.

To have free reign within the hearts of believers is Gods deepest desire. It's His will that all submit to His authority that we would live an abundant and fruitful life. The heart or breasts of believers are the center of our Christianity focused on faith and love.

It is the goodness and love of God that draws our hearts to repentance (Romans 2:4). His love for us while we were yet sinners draws our hearts to Him and causes us to declare Him Lord. We are saved by grace through faith. Faith and love grow together in us. As we read the Word and communicate with the Father, our faith grows, which causes us to see new things in Him. His goodness and love in showing us these greater things causes love and more faith to grow in us.

The cycle of growth in all believers is one of love and faith. During times of trial and pressure, our faith is tested and proven as we rest on His love and sheltering goodness. These trials and tests of faith, while we are sheltered in the love of God, grow us to develop deeper fruits of the Spirit. Our faith in Christ produces righteousness and the ability to stand without condemnation, but it is the love of God that allows us to rightly see the judgement and correction of God without fear of abandonment.

How did love and faith play a role in your salvation experience?

Read 1 Thessalonians 5:8

What is the significance of this breastplate being made of faith and love? How do these two protect our heart?

Read Ephesians 6:14

What is another attribute of this breastplate? How does this relate to faith and love?

Prayer: I thank you Jesus for your love and willingness to sacrifice yourself for me. I pray Holy Spirit that you would reveal even more of this love to me and show me the best way to share it with others. I praise you Lord for this love and faith which guards my heart and makes me strong enough to withstand the enemy. In Jesus' name. Amen.

Activation: Take the time today to reflect on your walk with God. If you have had any breakthroughs or testimonies during this study, write them down to share. Building up our faith often involves sharing the breakthrough and victory with others. Our victory can encourage others to seek the Lord for their own breakthrough. Be ready to share! We would love for you to share with us. Share your testimony of breakthrough. @discipleshiptr1

The Cross Supplied

Until the day breaks and the shadows flee away, I will get to the mountain of myrrh and the hill of frankincense.

The Song of Solomon 4:6

The only way shadows flee is for everything to be revealed in the light. Even those things which try to hide will be revealed in the light of the Son. While dark nights, tests, and trials, try to overpower and overshadow truths the light of the world reveals in us, we must encompass ourselves within the safety and security of our strong tower.

Even when we face difficult choices and circumstances, in Him we can do all things. Before this bride called out for her bridegroom to return to her, and she now takes the first steps toward Him. It is when we seek Him first in all things that we are victorious, because we are relying on His strength instead of our own. When we turn away from our own strength and rely on His, the yoke and burden are light (Matthew 11:28).

The first steps in times of trial should be toward this mountain of myrrh. This mountain scented with myrrh is the tabernacle in the desert which was anointed with oil of myrrh. The fragrance is pleasing to God, and is our life surrendered to His purpose and plan on the earth.

When we present ourselves, let it be scented with myrrh as Esther was presented, purified and living in her purpose (Esther 2:12).

The more we die to our own will the more we will see His resurrection life within us. Our purity as His bride is paramount. While we may feel overwhelmed by mountains of sacrifice, the hill of purity is easy to climb because He lives within us. Before the myrrh and frankincense were perfumes or drops of anointing oil, now they are mountains and hills. When we truly start to see the imperfections within us, the overwhelming work of the cross begins to show itself in the excess they provide.

What are the similarities and differences between sacrifice and purity?

Read 2 Corinthians 4:10

How does the life of Jesus manifest in believers?

Read 1 Corinthians 1:18

Why is the cross so foolish to the unsaved? How does a believer view the cross?

Prayer: Lord, I pray that You are glorified in my thoughts, actions, and words. Let all I am give You glory and honor. I pray that more of You would manifest in me. Let me see the world the way You see it. In Jesus' name. Amen.

Activation: Today step out of your comfort zone and ask the Lord for a word of encouragement for someone. Write it out and ask for His leading who you should give it to. Stepping out can be challenging. The Lord told me to write down a short verse about beauty from ashes and that I would know who I should share it with. I saw a young woman looking over beauty products at target and had the distinct impression she was the one to hand the card with the verse to. She was confused until I told her the Lord had pointed her out for an encouraging word. She read the card and burst into tears. Someone had just recently made a comment that hurt her feelings deeply, but the knowledge that God singled her out and called her beautiful changed her pain to joy.

Beauty Within

O my love, how beautiful you are! There is no flaw in you!

The Song of Solomon 4:7

Those things which the world sees as beautiful are not what the Lord sees as beautiful. The death of will and sacrifice of our desires are beautiful to our bridegroom. Notice how He says there is no spot *in* you. The outward appearance of men may fool many, but God knows the deep things within our hearts. He is calling the heart of this bride pure and clean.

This spotless life is brought to us only by the blood of our bridegroom which washes all who believe white as snow (Psalm 51:7). There is great power in the blood of Christ to wash and cleanse us. This washing by the Word and blood of Jesus cleanses our inner and outer man of impure thoughts and actions (1 John 1:7).

How does the blood of Christ cleanse your thoughts and actions?

Read 2 Peter 3:14 in the Amplified

How should we be found upon Christ's return? What state should be in?

Read 1 Corinthians 6:11

List the truths for believers found in this verse.

Prayer: Lord, You have made the heavens and the earth and all things in it. I thank You and praise You for making my heart Your home and my conscious clean. Help me speak with boldness and mercy and keep my heart from entertaining wicked things as I share Your name with the world. In Jesus' name. Amen.

Activation: The accuser tries time and again to remind us of our past failures, but in Christ we are not only cleansed of sin but also guilt. Have you felt accused lately? In your journal, write down what a free conscience looks like, and speak this over yourself.

Away to New Places

Come away with me from Lebanon, my [promised] bride, come with me from Lebanon. Depart from the top of Amana, from the peak of Senir and Hermon, from the lions' dens, from the mountains of the leopards.

The Song of Solomon 4:8

Again, the bridegroom calls her away from places she knows. Before He had called her away from the secluded places so he could see her clearly. Now He calls her away from Lebanon, the place of natural resources. The land of Lebanon was rich with wood for building, the spices of trade, and clear waters.

He is telling her to follow a path that will carry her away from the top of Amana, the mountain of support, and away from Hermon, to a new place in Him. Mt. Hermon has three summits of which two were within the realm of the tribe of Manasseh. Upon these two pinnacles Hermon and Senir, mountains and valleys of riches and resources were visible.

To understand this call, we must understand why Mt. Hermon is so important. Not only was this the highest point within the entire range of mountains, it is the northernmost point of the land given to the Israelites by God. The peaks, of Hermon are visible as far south as the Dead Sea. The mountain itself contains several peaks which all held a significant place in Israel's history.

The name Hermon is rooted in the word חרם haram which means 'two possible ways someone could go in a stage of transition'. This relates to stages of growth and how God uses us in differing ways dependent upon where we are in our walk with Him. It is His will that we move forward in His plan and purpose for us. This is why the bridegroom is calling her from this place of transition. It is His desire that she follow Him from this place to another where even more growth can occur.

It's also here upon Mt. Hermon that the Jordan River finds its source. The waters of the Jordan River were more than a geographic barrier. It was upon crossing it that the Israelites entered the Promised Land into the destiny God had shown His servants Moses and Abraham. Crossing it was a transition from the leadership of Moses to the leadership of Joshua.

When leaving Egypt behind, the children of Israel found themselves free of the bondage of slavery, but were in their minds very much slaves to the world. We can all be set free by the atoning blood of Jesus, but if our minds never renew to the truth of our victory, we still act as though the world is our master. It was only after a period of time in the wilderness and the passing of a generation that they found themselves able to enter the land that flowed with milk and honey.

The Word tells us that the natural experience of the children of Israel is a spiritual truth for us in Christ (1 Corinthians 10:9). We have been redeemed from the world typified by Egypt, and have a much greater testament that does not require death within the wilderness. We move by our bridegroom's grace out of the world and Egypt by His sacrifice.

There is more to our Christian life however than simply leaving the world. We are brought to the pinnacles of Mt. Hermon peaks to oversee the entirety of the promise. All the land would be spread out before you, and the truth of His place far above all rule and authority becomes evident.

How does the Lord address the bride in this verse? Has he called her by this title before?

Read 1 Corinthians 6:17

What happens when a person is joined to the Lord?

Read 1 Peter 3:21

What is the significance of a 'good and clear conscience' when serving the Father?

Read Deuteronomy 30:19

What are the possible ways we can 'go' in life? What is the significance of this being our choice?

Prayer: Father, I ask You sanctify my spirit, soul, and body. Search my heart and conscious and cleanse me of all unrighteousness. Help me cast out every evil thought, any anger, and pride. Let me be fully submitted to Your will. In Jesus' name. Amen.

Application: Every day we face choices. It's often difficult to stop and ask the Lord for direction for each and every choice set before us, but in the Word, we see Jesus only doing what the Father told Him to do. Practice asking God before doing anything today, and begin a habit of living in constant communication with the Father in Heaven.

Running the Race

You have ravished my heart and given me courage, my sister, my [promised] bride; you have ravished my heart and given me courage with one look from your eyes, with one jewel of your necklace.

The Song of Solomon 4:9

With just one look, the bridegroom is captivated by this bride and transported with love. She is leaving the security and comfort she is accustomed to and venturing onto the path He calls her to walk. This act of obedience to the will of the Father encourages both her and her bridegroom. How far will this sister follow? She is of the same Father, but she has something altogether unique no other can give, the pure affection of her heart.

These jewels on the necklace he gives her for the obedient actions done in this life. Before, the bridegroom stated she had adorned herself with jewels and asked her to buy from Him gold refined by fire. Now these treasures refined by fire are those things for which we receive rewards at the Judgement Seat of Christ (2 Corinthians 5:10).

The apostle John tells us "do not lose those things but that we would receive a full reward." There is no reward without earning it and trusting that He rewards those who diligently seek Him. When we seek after the heart of the Father we find we are all called. Paul calls this 'our race', and like every race there is a course to follow (Hebrews 12:1).

It's okay to seek the rewards of heaven; for it is by these actions he reminds us that our treasure should be stored in heaven. Living with eternity in mind in all that we say and do is to live for Christ. Again, this judgment is not for sin as that was borne on the cross, instead, it is a decision based on what we were called to do, and what was really done in our lives.

What are your first thoughts when you hear 'Judgement Seat of Christ?'

What two things about the bride have ravished the Lord's heart?

Read Luke 11:34

What is this single or clear eye?

Read 1 Corinthians 3:11-15 in the Amplified

What foundation has already been laid? What can be built upon it? How is the workmanship 'tested'? If the workmanship passes the test, what happens?

Prayer: Thank you Jesus for being the firm foundation upon which I can stand. Let my life and all I do build your church upon that foundation, and let my eyes never leave the goal you have for me in Jesus' name. Amen.

Activation: In Habakkuk chapter 2, the Lord told the prophet to write the vision so it would be plainly read by the people. Having vision and goals is part of God's design. You've asked for direction and for plans before. Take time today to write out the vision and put it somewhere you'll see it often. If you prefer, draw a picture or make a collage. Whatever it is that motivates you to continue on a daily basis reaching for those goals is best. Remember to praise God when each and every goal is achieved.

Kindred

How beautiful is your love, my sister, my [promised] bride! How much better is your love than wine! And the fragrance of your ointments than all spices!

The Song of Solomon 4:10

The bridegroom changes his compliment. Earlier He called her beautiful with dove's eyes, now it's her love for Him that's beautiful. She is of the same Father and also is His bride.

Her love is better than wine! In Jesus's time it was common for the bridegroom's Father to choose a bride for his son. When a suitable match was found, the bridegroom would journey to the woman's home. In the presence of her Father he would pour a wine offering in the Kiddush, or sanctification cup, of his Father's house. This sanctification cup was the same cup used for Shabbat and Passover by the Father of the house when reciting the blessings.

After filling the Kiddush, the bridegroom would raise it in his right hand and declare his desire for the woman as a wife. After taking a sip, he would place it in front of her and wait. If she took a sip, it showed her willingness to enter into the union of betrothal. If she didn't, the wine would be poured out.

If she chose to enter the union, a celebration would commence, and a mohar, or bride price, would be paid. The bride price would be paid to her family, but this money belonged to the bride. The payment set her free from her family and gave her means to follow the instruction of her bridegroom. This union of betrothal was so binding, a divorce was necessary to end it.

When the bridegroom returned to his Father's house, he left his bride to be with a gift as a reminder of His future return to her. Jesus states in John 16 that it was better He leave and go to the Father so that the Holy Spirit could come. This same Spirit that anointed Jesus now anoints us with a fragrance that is perceptible to those around us. This scent isn't perceived by eyes or ears, bringing to our remembrance the verse in 1 Corinthians 2:9-10: "But as it is written, Eye hath not seen, nor ear heard, neither have entered into the heart of man, the things which God hath prepared for them that love him. But God hath revealed them unto us by his Spirit: for the Spirit searcheth all things, yea, the deep things of God."

This gift of the Holy Spirit is that awesome gift prepared for those who love Him. Only with the leading, guiding, and counsel of the Spirit can we accomplish all the things that God has set before us. The Holy Spirit searches the deep things of God and reveals them to our spirit so we may be comforted with a continual flow of love, grace, and understanding from Heaven.

Once the bridegroom returned to his Father's house, the building would commence. It was common in Hebrew culture to add a room onto his Father's house. Only when the Father determined the room ready was the son allowed to return for his bride. The wait was one of expectancy rather than despair, for at any moment her bridegroom could come and collect her.

During this time of betrothal, her vows demanded that she prepare herself for his arrival, and she would daily consecrate and purify herself while making her wedding garments. Then she would hear a cry 'behold the bridegroom comes!' and loud shofar would blow through the streets. Her wedding day had arrived.

How can one remain faithful to the Lord when we don't see Him? How does your relationship with Jesus change when you view it as a marriage union? Is this different than a union with a Savior? Why or why not?

Read 2 Corinthians 2:14-16

What is the fragrance the bride shares? To whom does it appeal? How does it affect those around her?

Read 1 Corinthians 6:19-20

How do we bring honor and glory to God in our body?

Read Isaiah 62:3-5

Describe how the Lord sees His beloved.

Prayer: Father, sanctify my heart and make it clean. Cleanse my thoughts of all unrighteousness and help me focus on the soon arrival of my bridegroom. Help me stay pure in thought and deed and help me to continually give glory to my savior in Jesus' name. Amen.

Application: The wait for our Lord's return is one of expectancy. While many believe His arrival is far off and don't give heed to discipleship, we must focus daily on our kingdom work. Our daily sacrifice of laying aside our will and doing the work we are called to do takes focus and unwavering faith. Today, take time to focus on your bridegroom's return and the joy of the marriage supper.

Sweet Words from Our Lips

Your lips, O my [promised] bride, drop honey as the honeycomb; honey and milk are under your tongue. And the odor of your garments is like the odor of Lebanon.

The Song of Solomon 4:11

These lips that once were threads of scarlet are now even sweeter to the taste of the bridegroom. While sacrifice is a part of her life, abundance is now being shown in her words. For out of the heart the mouth speaks, and while the death and burial of our savior brought us victory, we must move past the cross into His resurrection and the abundant life provided by sacrifice.

The milk and honey found in the land of promise was a sign not only of the land's abundance but also its assurance of rest and comfort. Now that the Israelites had passed through the wilderness they were entering a land where there would always be more than enough. The transition for the children of Israel is of great spiritual significance for believers. John the Baptist ate honey and locusts as a sign of transition from a time of judgement and oppression, disaster, and affliction to a time of spiritual sweetness and abundance in Christ (Matthew 3:4).

Milk is the first food for those that are new and growing. As time passes and we mature, our foods change. This milk no longer satisfies our growth, nor can it provide complete nourishment for us. Once you've correlated this to growth in the Spirit, you see it translates into honey. The addition of other sources of nourishment enables us to grow as we are called to do. For the children of Israel, it was the addition of honey to the manna from heaven that made it pleasant to the palate, but it wasn't until they had learned to trust God for their daily supply that they entered the land of promise.

Garments fragrant with frankincense are those worn by this bride on her wedding day. They are the garments of holy righteousness purchased by her bridegroom on Calvary. At this great marriage supper, we will celebrate in new garments with our bridegroom in the presence of the Father. It is only these garments that make us fit for the Father's house and our bridegroom's sacrifice.

What is the significance of living in resurrection life? How might this be different than living focused on the cross? How should we live with both the cross and resurrection in mind?

Read Proverbs 24:12-14

What does the one who eats honey and the honeycomb gain from the Lord?

Read Ezekiel 16

Describe God's faithfulness toward an unfaithful people. In what ways do we as brides of Christ need to view our marriage covenant? What wayward wanderings should we be mindful of?

Read Deuteronomy 8:7-9

What is our 'Good Land' as believers in Christ? What signs of this 'Good land' have we studied so far?

Prayer: I praise You Lord for Your faithfulness even when I am unfaithful. I pray that You would strengthen me through the Holy Spirit to stand firm and not let the fleshly things of the world overshadow your presence. Help my eyes stay focused and never wander from your goodness in Jesus' name. Amen.

Application: Every time we submit new areas of our lives to the Lord, He responds with joy and eagerness. Are there any areas of your life you still feel the need to control or manage? Spend time speaking with the Lord today about how you can give control of those areas of life to Him. Write down your thoughts and feelings in your journal.

A Garden of Satisfaction

A garden enclosed and barred is my sister, my [promised] bride—a spring shut up, a fountain sealed.

The Song of Solomon 4:12

There is nothing within this walled garden that does not belong to Him. Every fruit borne out of her comes forth for His benefit, and the walls of defense that are in place guard her from the thief who seeks to steal and destroy. This barred door is guarded so that she may give all her attention to the inner growth necessary to serve her King. It is only He who holds the key to this barrier.

Within the garden lies a spring of water. Springs were plentiful within the land of promise, and the brooks and springs which flowed from the hills were fed by water deep within the earth. It is from the spring within us that the water of life, which is Jesus, flows from us.

When we shut this spring up, it hampers our growth and prevents us from sharing this water with others. Though the springs of Israel were precious, the spring of living water within us is even more so, for it quenches a thirst in people for eternity. This is why the spring within us carries a seal.

Seals announced ownership, and whoever tampered with what was sealed knew whom they would be held accountable for the tampering. We as believers have been sealed by the Holy Spirit and separated unto Him. The enemy of our soul knows who rules and reigns in our hearts by this seal upon us.

Adam and Eve were created and placed in a garden to tend it for the Lord. How does this original intent of God correspond to this bride being called a garden enclosed?

Read John 7:37-38

How does this water flow from us? Where does it originate?

Read 2 Corinthians 1:22 in the Amplified

Why were believers sealed? Why was the Holy Spirit given to believers? In your own words, explain what that promise would be.

Read Genesis 3:8

Why is the Lord walking through the garden significant? What was this garden's purpose? Do you believe the Lord enjoys the garden in your heart?

Prayer: Lord, shine a light into my heart and search it for any untruth and reveal to me the truth. Let my heart be a place where You abide and do so with joy. I pray that You make Yourself known to me in a deeper way and help me navigate the world with Your wisdom and grace in Jesus' name. Amen.

Application: Bring your journal with you and take a walk through a garden or park. Write down all the things you enjoy and ask the Lord to reveal why you enjoy them. Take time to ask the Father what He enjoys in your heart.

Fragrance of the Spirit

Your shoots are an orchard of pomegranates or a paradise with precious fruits, henna with spikenard plants,

The Song of Solomon 4:13

Tender shoots that break through the earth are beautiful in the sight of our Lord. It is the sign of new growth and flourishing life. The shoots grow and mature into the orchards of fruit promised, believers in the Word. An important realization is that the fruit produced for its owner, the one who enclosed it and holds the key to its barred door. He set a seal upon our hearts and called us His own.

The precious fruits are not actual fruits one might consume in the flesh, but rather they are the fruits of the spirit. These fruits were already borne in our spirit when we gave our lives over to Christ. When we understand to grow in the Spirit is to rest on the promises of God, we grow these tender fruits to feed others.

"But the fruit of the Spirit [the result of His presence within us] is love [unselfish concern for others], joy, [inner] peace, patience [not the ability to wait, but how we act while waiting], kindness, goodness, faithfulness, gentleness, self-control. Against such things there is no law." Galatians 5:22-23 AMP

Pomegranate, henna, and spikenard together remind us our bridegroom is pointing to our growth and value in Him. The pomegranate signifies the pure and Godly thoughts a transformed mind brings. Henna and spikenard remind us of His wounds and fragrant anointing oil, signifying the price paid when He gave His life on the cross. It was not without the shedding of His blood that we could overcome and the price for sin be paid. Now as we charge forward in all the other attributes He notes, let us keep this as our remembrance.

Henna blooms were used to describe the bridegroom in Chapter 1. What is the significance of the Lord using that same flower to describe the bride?

Read Philippians 4:7-8

Many of the fruits of the Spirit are listed in these verses. How do these fruits begin to appear? What is the importance of thinking in developing something from our spirit?

Read Colossians 1:9

Why is spiritual wisdom and discernment important to believers? How does this wisdom and discernment help us in our walk with God?

Read 2 Corinthians 3:18

When we gain wisdom and discernment of the Word, what is happening in us?

Prayer: Lord, like Solomon, I pray for wisdom and discernment of spiritual things. Open my eyes to the truth of who I am in Christ and the authority I have over the enemy in His holy name. Give me the wisdom to seek Your face first in all circumstances and praise You in every situation in Jesus' name. Amen.

Application: We have studied the fruits of the Spirit previously and evaluated how they were growing in our lives. Today, go back to that page of your journal and update it with your growth and progress in all the fruits. Ask the Father for any areas you can focus on and grow this week.

A Precious Spice

Spikenard and saffron, calamus and cinnamon, with all trees of frankincense, myrrh, and aloes, with all the chief spices.

The Song of Solomon 4:14

Saffron was precious in the ancient world. It takes 75,000 flowers to produce just one pound of saffron. Workers gently pluck the stigmas of the crocus flower by hand and dry them immediately in a kiln. This extra care tells us it is a precious spice, but the part that is gathered tells us so much more.

Stigmas of a flower are found within the petals. As the flower matures, these stigmas receive pollen from the plant which leads to the growth of seeds within the fruit. The stigma does not do any work of its own to capture the pollen; it's just receptive to it when the pollen lands on its surface. We too must be receptive to the direction of the Lord when it comes. It's not necessary for us to work and strain to seek out His will; we must be receptive when it comes.

Fields of crocus where the saffron is gathered are ringed by small kilns which are carefully tended. Once the stigmas are picked, it's necessary to quickly lay them out to dry in these kilns. If any began to mold, the whole batch would be lost, and if any fire burned too hot, the stigmas would scorch and be bitter. The Lord is pointing us to an important truth we must ask ourselves. What happens when we are subject to trials and tests by fire?

Do we linger, afraid of the fire, unsure of His faithfulness only to grow foul when we see opportunity has passed? Do we wither and become bitter when we experience the fire? Are we preserved as a precious spice when we seek Him for truth and timing, and flavor all we mingle with?

This precious spice is paired with the fragrant spikenard. The joining of these two amplifies to us the precious nature of our Lord's death and sacrifice. It was a carefully orchestrated event and was a precious gift indeed. Its timing, execution, and process was clearly foretold by prophets for centuries. He is the author of hope.

Calamus, or fragrant cane, comes from the Hebrew word meaning 'upright and balanced'. Just as we are upright before the Lord, we must also be balanced. No longer do we rely on our own works, but we rely on the finished work of our Savior and are receptive to Him when He calls.

Cinnamon was also a spice added to the anointing oil of the tabernacle and was imported along with calamus along the Silk Road from India. How awesome is our God that His anointing oil comes from people all over the earth.

Psalm 45 celebrates the king's marriage, but this is not a song for Solomon. This psalm is a celebration for the King of Kings; it is for that great wedding day when the marriage supper of the lamb gathers all believers together in a great celebration of our Lord. The aloes and myrrh perfume His garments with what is called the oil of jubilation. This joyous fragrance permeates the senses and turns our hearts to Him. These garments are of His resurrection, for John tells us Nicodemus brought the myrrh and aloes to anoint his body before burial.

List all the spices that grow in the garden of the bride's soul. How many individual spices are listed? How many fruits of the Spirit are listed in Galatians?

Read Psalm 45

What passages stand out to you the most in this Psalm? What instruction do you take away from that verse?

Read Exodus 30:23-30

What were these spices used for? Who was anointed with this oil?

Read Revelation 5:8

How do your prayers correlate to this fragrance offered before the Lord?

Read Leviticus 2:1

What is the grain offering symbolic of? What is the significance of the frankincense being offered with the grain?

Prayer: Thank You Lord for preserving me even when I experience trials and tests in life. I pray for patience and Your supernatural covering so that I may endure and stand fast in my faith. I pray Holy Spirit for Your comfort when I am uncomfortable in Jesus' name. Amen.

Application: It's often difficult to see God's hand while we experience tests and trials in life. Take time today to look back on some hard situations you've experienced and ask God to reveal to you how He was helping you through. Write this in your journal and add it to your testimony.

A Garden for the Lord

You are a fountain [springing up] in a garden, a well of living waters, and flowing streams from Lebanon.

The Song of Songs 4:15

Deep within the hearts of every believer lay wells of living water. It's when we begin to pour this water on others that they flow and spring up from within. The life of our bridegroom poured out must also pour out of our hearts towards those who need the refreshing living water. It is the only source that gives life. One might say they have experienced the depths of

Jesus Christ, but the source of these springs is hidden deep. Any water we see or partake of from this spring is new and wondrous.

In Genesis we see Rebekah, whose name means supported one, draw upon a well to bless the traveler Eliezer, meaning God is help and support, and his camels sent by Abraham. By drawing on the well, she not only obeyed the Lord, but shifted the entire course of her life. It was the servants answer to prayer for his master's bride-to-be, and it was the course which the Father had laid before her to take.

When we realize this well in the natural world sustained her and those she traveled with across the desert, we see an even greater truth of this well's place in life. It is from the well we are sustained through difficult journeys, and it is from the well we source our supply as we run our course. Just as Rebecca labored to water the camels that would carry her to her bridegroom, we too must draw on this well to nourish those who walk alongside us as we live the Christian life.

The land of Lebanon was known as the land of white-capped peaks. From Mount Hermon, many rivers and streams find their source, bringing life and refreshing to the land south of it. The streams that flow from this place shadow those same streams that flow from our innermost being. These streams get their source from that which is pure in our hearts, which is Christ.

How does the Lord help us draw water from the well inside us?

Read Psalm 36:8-9

Where does the abundance originate? What does it give to those who partake?

Read John 4:10-11

Explain the significance of the Samaritan woman's statement that 'the well is deep'.

Prayer: Thank You Father for the gift of the Holy Spirit to lead and guide me in all truth. Let my heart be ready to receive the instruction and direction the Spirit brings and let me be quick to follow it in Jesus' name. Amen.

Application: Ask the Lord today for a word of encouragement for a fellow believer. Trust the Holy Spirit to reveal what you should share with them, and be ready to deliver this encouragement when called. Share your experience with us and encourage others who are learning to hear the Spirit! @Discipleshiptr1

Wind of the Spirit

[You have called me a garden, she said] Oh, I pray that the [cold] north wind and the [soft] south wind may blow upon my garden, which its spices may flow out [in abundance for you in whom my soul delights]. Let my beloved come into his garden and eat its choicest fruits.

The Song of Solomon 4:16

Winds from the north are strong and cool. In Israel, they are winds that often bring rain and the cooler winter weather The south winds, by contrast, frequently bring the heat and dryness of the desert regions. The bride is asking these winds to blow upon the garden of her heart. The bride is asking the Lord to use all circumstances, refreshing rains and dry heat, to grow her and show the world the goodness of Christ.

Encourage, remind, and make aware the need for fruitfulness in her spirit. 'Grow,' she says, 'and bring hope and joy for all those whom the Lord sees fit to share in the fruits I have grown, for this is my service and my joy'.

The choicest fruits are most desirable to the palate. They are free of spot and blemish just as our Lamb was spotless for us. In Leviticus, we are called to make sacrifice of the fruits of the tree. These choice fruits are presented before the Lord as our tithe or our acknowledgement of His Lordship in our lives. When we live with the winds of the spirit encouraging and reminding us of the truth, we produce these choice fruits for our bridegroom's glory.

Wind is not visible, but its effects are easily seen. Are there any instances in your life where the effects of God's workings were visible without seeing what He was doing? How did this experience help grow your faith?

Read Psalm 19:11-14

How might these verses compare to the bride's request for the north and south winds to blow?

Read Matthew 13:58

What was the result of the unbelief of those in Nazareth? How can unbelief affect our prayers and walk with God?

Read Romans 4:19-21

What is the result of unwavering faith? What might cause your faith to waiver?

Read Hebrews 4:10-12

How does one grow in faith that does not waiver?

Prayer: Father, I pray that my heart would always be grounded in the truth of Your goodness. Let my heart not falter or waiver when I don't understand, but remind me You are the Creator of all things and my end is in Your hands. I praise You in the midst of trail and thank You for the Rock which gives me a firm foundation in Jesus' name. Amen.

Activation: Take time to think about how God has shown His love and care for the small details of your life. Where has God shown Himself in those details? Write down all the ways your life has been influenced for the kingdom.

CHAPTER 5

The Mountains and Valleys of Love

A Garden of Enjoyment

I have come into my garden, my sister, my [promised] bride; I have gathered my myrrh with my balsam and spice [from your sweet words I have gathered the richest perfumes and spices]. I have eaten my honeycomb with my honey; I have drunk my wine with my milk. Eat, O friends [feast on, O revelers of the palace; you can never make my lover disloyal to me]! Drink, yes, drink abundantly of love, O precious one [for now I know you are mine, irrevocably mine! With his confident words still thrilling her heart, through the lattice she saw her shepherd turn away and disappear into the night].

The Song of Songs 5:1

This garden, which grows the fruits of the Spirit for His glory, is a place of enjoyment and plenty. He enters and partakes of the fruits and the spices which fragrance our inner sanctification. The myrrh, balsam, and spice He gathers from our words are fulfilling. Here those precious fragrant words are compared to the honeycomb and honey which sustain, and the wine which pours out and symbolizes our sacrifice of self and life yielded to the cross of Christ.

Our bridegroom enters and partakes when invited. Often, we mistake His absence in our lives for His wandering, when truly it is our hearts that wander from Him. Spiritual maturity is living a life that continually requests the presence of our Savior. It's only when we yield to His continual influence that we are able to grow in abundance in our Christian life.

In the seventh chapter of Isaiah, we see the prophet speaking of Jesus where he mentions that He will eat butter, curds, and honey when He is old enough to choose good over evil. In the same manner, we must partake of the spiritual blessing our new wine provides, and provide milk to those who grow up under our care and influence.

This bride quenched the dryness of her soul with the living water. Everyone in this world is perishing from drought in the spirit until they are connected to the living water that can satisfy. Once the Lord supplies life via the water of life that satisfies our soul, we see there is nourishment in that life. This is the milk we progress to as we grow in Christ.

We are told to crave the pure milk of the word. It is by the Word and through the Word that we are nourished in our spirits and grow to maturity as believers. The Word of God is alive and changes thoughts and beliefs. There is even more for the bride to experience from here.

If we could only secure this in our minds and hearts without fail. The bread of life who is Christ, the water of life flowing from the Father, the wine of joy unspeakable, and the milk of nourishing truths are priceless. Yet they are all made available to us without cost. These priceless gifts are a perfect display of the Father's love for us. Everything we need in this life is provided for us. Health and wholeness are ours in Christ. Joy and inner peace that are not dependent on circumstances are ours.

This garden of our hearts belongs to the Lord, but we see He invites others to partake of the fruits it produces. Who do you believe these 'friends' might be? How do the fruits our lives produce nourish them?

Read Isaiah 55:1-2
How is it possible to buy grain, wine, and milk without money? What is the result of eating these things bought from the Lord?

Read 1 Peter 2:2

If pure milk is the Word of God how do we purchase it? What happens when we do?

Read Proverbs 16:24

How do pleasant words heal our body?

Read Isaiah 53:10b-11

What are the fruits of Jesus' travail?

Prayer: Heavenly Father, I pray for Your Holy Spirit to plant and develop in my heart the Fruits of the Spirit. Let me always keep You first in my heart and mind. Work in me Holy Spirit to nourish and equip those who see my life as Your written epistle. In Jesus name, Amen.

Activation: While witnessing to individuals, there may be times when your full testimony isn't the most effective way to share Christ. Sometimes the people we engage with share their hurts or their shortcomings with us out of frustration or a desire for answers. Take some time today to think about areas (especially concerning Fruits of the Spirit) where God has shown a mighty work in renewing you. How would you share this awesome growth God initiated in your life? Someone may need to hear this testimony of hope from you!

He Stands at the Door

I went to sleep, but my heart stayed awake. [I dreamed that I heard] the voice of my beloved as he knocked [at the door of my mother's cottage]. Open to me, my sister, my love, my dove, my spotless one [he said], for I am wet with the [heavy] night dew; my hair is covered with it.

The Song of Songs 5:2

Our spirits are always in communion with the Father. Once we close our natural eyes and let the world fall away, we will hear his voice clearly. The distractions of this life often keep us in a state of uncertainty. The Holy Spirit desires that we all awaken our hearts to His voice. We must allow all distractions to fall away and hear our bridegroom's voice and the truths that He shares.

The truth we have seen so far is our King first takes possession of our hearts when we call upon Him as Lord. From this place of enthronement in us, we gain revelation of His grace and mercy displayed on the cross. However, the cross was not the end of this work, for three days later He rose in victory over sin and death. This resurrection power and might displays that God is the author of new creations.

The bride is His spotless dove, a new creation in Christ, and she perceives the Spirit of Truth. The dove is symbolic of the Holy Spirit, which searches out the deep knowledge that is found within the Spirit of the Father. This Holy Spirit sees and perceives knowledge and mysteries that are kept hidden from the enemy of our soul, and reveals them to us. As with all gifts from the Father, we must be receptive. One truth that evades many is that to fully experience the resurrection life of Christ, we too must become partakers of His sufferings.

In Genesis 27, we find the story of Jacob and Esau. Though the blessing of his Father Isaac should have been given to his brother Esau, Jacob was the recipient of the blessing. While he was speaking his blessing, Isaac notes the scent of Esau(Jacob) to be like the aroma of the fields that the Lord blessed. He asks the Lord for dew from Heaven to water the land in which he lives so that the land would be fertile and produce an abundant harvest.

The Lord calls His bride His love, His dove, and His spotless one. We are the recipient of the Lord's favor and we see the blessing of the dew upon us. The heavy dews in the land of Israel provided necessary water for all the plants during times of drought and heat. At some point in our walk with the Lord we will experience trials of heat and dryness.

Dew is the blessing from above as well as the blessing of a king upon his subjects. In Isaiah 26, we see dew is what brings the dead to life. It is symbolic of our newness of life in Christ and the manna of heaven that fell in the wilderness.

He stands at the door and is asking to be let in. Every day we must decide to allow the Lord's presence and influence in our lives. Do we still earnestly desire Him? Are we still seeking His wisdom and guidance in our lives? It is imperative that we keep the Lord in the first place of our hearts. We don't want to become lukewarm in our desire for Him.

Dew does not fall in the light of day. It is only when we are outdoors in the night that our bridegroom's hair could become damp. How true that it is easy to live in the light of day, but to reach those who do not yet know him we must venture outside in the night of another person's life.

When the Israelites stood before the Jordan, Moses blessed the nation after his commission of Joshua to lead them into the promised land. As we look closer at this psalm, we find a symmetry which one must not overlook. Moses correlates the falling of various types of precipitation upon the land and people as a refreshing fall of words upon their ears and hearts. As we face trials, let this gentle dew of the Word fall upon our ears and hearts.

What does Jesus call the bride in this verse? What is the significance of these titles?

Read John 10:27

What is the promise of this verse to the followers of Christ?

Read Revelation 3:20

If we answer and open to Jesus when He asks to enter what is the promise He gives?

Read Deuteronomy 32:1-2

Describe the significance of the phrase 'my speech distill as the dew'.

Read Hosea 14:4-5

The Lord says He will be like the dew. Describe all the things He does for the people.

Read 1 Corinthians 7:23

What is Paul trying to convey in this verse saying we are slaves to Christ?

Prayer: Lord, I pray that You would purify my heart and motives. Search my heart and change what needs to be changed, and pour out a refreshing upon my heart and mind that I would know and understand the peace of Christ in greater measure. I thank You that I am like the tree planted by rivers of water and bear fruit in season. In Jesus' name, Amen.

Application: All too often we neglect the refreshing necessary to ground us in the person of Christ. We scurry about doing the work of the kingdom and forsake the King. Take time today to refresh yourself in the Word and prayer. Ask the Lord for a personal refreshing that you would continue in His will and perfect plan.

Resurrection Life, Shown Forth

[But weary from a day in the vineyards, I had already sought my rest] I had put off my garment—how could I [again] put it on? I had washed my feet—how could I [again] soil them?

The Song of Songs 5:3

Even though we may tend the vines and branches of the church, how often do we tax ourselves doing works? So many believers find themselves suffering under stress and toils of works within the body they neglect the greatest work. It is not for us to avoid those things that God appointed for us to do, but how often do we find ourselves saying yes to things just to do them? We wash our own feet with self-righteousness but it was our Lord who washed the disciple's feet.

In this life, it's difficult to understand the importance of a life surrendered. To follow the example of Jesus is to do and say nothing outside what the Father would have us say or do. These works that Paul in the book of Corinthians calls worthless, keep many from following the true works they are called to do.

In our weariness, we find ourselves saying no to the call of our bridegroom. Why would we wish to defile ourselves with the world? We've put off our garment of a priest to serve other believers and taken off the shoes meant to share the gospel of piece to warm a seat in the pews.

Underneath the masks we all wear are the truths we cannot ignore. Whether they be masks of shame due to rampant sin in our lives, masks of prosperity when our souls cry out for enough to feed our families, or masks of joy covering for anxiety because we have not approached the Father with our troubles, we must all face the truth of our own selfishness.

The most destructive mask is one of apathy. We know our own salvation and rest in its assurance of eternity with the Father. Instead of our reliance on His wisdom and strength, we feel we have no need of the blessings only He provides. Why ask for healing when we have doctors? Why pray for provision when I have a job? Why pray in faith for another when they can pray for themselves? We find ourselves indifferent to the sufferings of others, and we neglect to see the horrible truth of where we really rest.

In resurrection life, the sufferings we face are more than the outward sufferings of a life lived surrendered to God. Looking to the cross, many see its sufferings, redemption, or identity, but few look to the cross and see its shame. We fear looking like fools for Christ so we back away from the call to follow. This path the bride is now being called to is one of inward sanctification.

To glory in the shame of the cross is to submit our spirit to the Holy Spirit. Our hearts will begin to respond to sin the same way the Father's heart responds. We will feel the rejection and rebellion in the hearts of men and begin to travail in prayer for their souls. Our life becomes His life, and we will become even more like Him.

Have you experienced persecution for being a follower of Christ? What was your reaction to it? Did you shy away from sharing Christ after that event?

Read Isaiah 53:11
What did the travail of Christ bring forth?

Read Revelation 3:16-17
What might lukewarm spirituality look like?

Ephesians 4:22-24

What has the bride already accomplished in following her bridegroom? Why is this spiritual progress so significant?

Prayer: Father, let Your Word be a light unto my feet and lamp unto my path. Let my heart be humble before You as I seek Your Word for wisdom and understanding. I pray for clarity in mind so I would know Your voice and direction. Let me always ask You before I move so I am in perfect alignment with You. In Jesus name, amen.

Activation: It's easy to lose sight of the many wonderful ways the Father uses a willing vessel. Today I'd like to encourage you to begin a journal of all the amazing encounters God uses you to share His love and mercy. Looking back at these entries will truly humble any heart. For it's not by our strength, but by His grace that we are able to turn the hearts of the lost toward the lover of their soul.

The Lord Beckons

My beloved put in his hand by the hole of the door, and my heart was moved for him.

The Song of Songs 5:4

The Lord is amazing in His ways. Every word and action has a meaning and purpose. While we may view this verse lightly, there is great wisdom from the Lord for us here. Many of us move without meaning and lean without understanding, but here the Lord is exemplifying in this passage an important correlation.

This hole by the door to some may be the keyhole, or even an intricate lock system commonly used in Solomon's day, but to understand the deeper significance, let us allow the word of God to expound upon the word *chowr,* translated hole.

This first usage of this word is in 1 Samuel 14:11. In this passage, we see the Philistines taunting Jonathan while the army of Israel emerges from the holes in which they have hidden. Often when we view our position in light of natural circumstances, we hide ourselves because all seems overwhelming.

It is easy to see the opposition arrayed against us, and it's difficult to see or feel the forces that are at our backs. We hide ourselves in our holes, waiting for a sign of divine providence, but we fail to recognize what that providence would be or how it might look. The bride has been called to join in the Lord's suffering, and this extending of His hand is that providence.

We often bemoan our fate when we see the enemy arrayed ready to fight and ruin us. Whether it be slander against us for our stand with Jesus or some inner desire that is in opposition to the plan of the Father, we must stand and open ourselves to his survey of our hearts. This is the true blessing of life that the Holy Spirit comes in to search our hearts and empower us.

The word blessed is often misunderstood by believers today. We feel that blessing from the Father is bestowed in final form in our lives, but we see in the Word this is not true. In Genesis, we see that the blessing of the Lord upon Adam and Eve is one of multiplication. The Father never placed the things which would bless them in front of them, but told them to fill the whole earth.

Our blessing from above is one of empowerment to prosper and increase. Bringing increase to the kingdom means working with God according to His plans. The bridegroom is called again to go forth from the place she is hiding and comfortable. Why? It's necessary for her blessings to tend the garden and bring forth the kingdom. If she chooses to do otherwise, her life will stagnate.

The Lord is calling to the bride by extending His hand. Explain how this posture of our Lord is encouraging and comforting to you.

Read the account of Jesus calling Peter to discipleship in Luke 5:1-11.

What is the first act of obedience from Peter?

Allowing the Lord to take use of his vessel for teaching, Peter is then asked to cast his net. What is his response?

What was Peter's reward for following the instructions of Jesus?

What are our rewards for following His instruction?

Jesus later tells Peter He will make him a fisher of men. Think about the implications of this story and how it applies to sharing the Gospel. Write down your thoughts.

Prayer: Lord, as I step out in faith, I pray now for boldness. Let me never waiver in following Your will no matter where it takes me. Help me remember the truth that He who is in me is greater than anyone in the world. I will continue to shout Your glory and majesty so my heart would never forget You, Lord, hold the seas in Your hand. In Jesus name, amen.

Activation: Is there a person you've been timid sharing your faith with? Ask the Lord for an opportunity to step out in faith with boldness. Ask Him for words to speak, a prayer to offer, a testimony to share and to see doors open before you. Don't forget to write these amazing encounters in your new journal!

Pass Over

I rose up to open for my beloved, and my hands dripped with myrrh and my fingers with liquid [sweet-scented] myrrh, [which he had left] upon the handles of the bolt.

The Song of Songs 5:5

The word translated liquid or sweet scented here is *abar*. It is used most often translated pass over, pass through, or even set apart. It is the same word the Lord uses in Exodus to describe His Passover of the Israelites the night of the first-born slaughter. This pass over myrrh was upon the bolt of the door as the bride-to-be rose. The same area of the door the Israelites were to paint with the blood of the Lamb in Egypt. The significance of the blood upon the door kept the destroyer from coming in. Even when she neglects His call, her bridegrooms call his blood is a shield for her.

There is a certain assurance in our salvation and the eternal destination of our spirits. However, we must also understand that in our lives now on the earth we are responsible to complete the race set before us. Many find comfort in the salvation but deny the greater truth that in this life we have been bought with a price. This price is our acceptable service to the furthering of our Father's kingdom.

Read the account of the first Passover in Exodus 12:1-27

What is the first commandment the Lord gives Moses? Why do you believe God chose to change the Hebrew calendar?

What were the stipulations on the lamb chosen for the sacrifice? When was the lamb slaughtered? How was it to be consumed?

Where was the blood placed? What was this a sign of? Who was it for?

How long were the Israelites to honor the Lord with a Passover celebration? How long did the celebration last?

What plant did the Israelites use to place the blood on the posts? Read Psalm 51:7 and explain the significance of this verse.

Prayer: I thank You, Lord, that I am set apart for Your purpose. Help my heart and mind stay focused on Your plan for me and not be distracted by things and people who would pull me from Your love. In Jesus name, amen.

Activation: To be fully set apart, we can no longer conform to this world. Early in my Christian life I lived a life partially dedicated to God and partially dedicated to my way. There came a time in my life when I heard the Father speaking to me about something, and I ignored Him. It took months for me to finally relent and get rid of what was, unknowing to me, causing my faith to waiver. Is there something God has spoken to you about? Have you ignored Him too? Take the steps today to set your heart apart for Him.

Respond with Faith

I opened for my beloved, but my beloved had turned away and withdrawn himself, and was gone! My soul went forth [to him] when he spoke, but it failed me [and now he was gone]! I sought him, but I could not find him; I called him, but he gave me no answer.

The Song of Songs 5:6

The same language used here, turned away and withdrawn, is used in Jeremiah when the prophet asks Israel how long they would continue to backslide and turn from His word and promises. The work of the enemy of our soul is always to kill the Christ in us. When we submit ourselves to his control and allow the world's cares, worries, and the sins of our flesh to disobey the Lord we see the effects as separation from the Father. This is what our betrothed is now seeing.

Again, she was called forth, but she allowed her cares of the world and what others would think of her to hold her back. She allowed her exhausting toil to bring her to a place of apathy in her own life. Her soul went forth to the Lord, as she knew it was necessary to follow Him, but the strength to follow through failed her. She had bathed herself after a toiling day and was tired, but her life should have been at rest in Christ. He is the source of her peace of mind.

So overwhelming are these cares and thoughts that even as she gets up and finds Him gone, she can't find him. How could this be? As believers in Christ, we have the promise that he will never leave us nor forsake us.

Even in the state of guilt and shame, the promises of God are of restoration and prosperity, the day when the law will be written on hearts and not on stone. It is the beginning of a time where this bride must walk by faith and not by sight. We often traverse difficulties in life, feeling as though there is no end in sight, or that the Lord is not with us to guide us through. These tests and trials we face strengthen and allow further growth in our lives, and through it all He is with us.

Read James 1:2

How can one count it joy to face tests and trials? What is the significance of the word 'when'?

Read James 1:13

Who brings the tests and trials of faith?

Read Job 1:5;8-11

What does the Lord say about Job? What is Satan's accusation? Why is all Job has in Satan's hand?

Read Matthew 27:46

When God's presence departed because the weight of sin was upon Him what did Jesus cry out? How does this suffering of our Lord encourage your pursuit of God's will for you?

Prayer: Lord, when I don't understand and answers fail me, lead and guide me in Your grace and mercy. I pray that You would give me a greater revelation of Your love that I would obey and walk knowing You are good and the God who is compassionate. In Jesus name, amen.

Application: The cares of this world are difficult to set aside. All believers have spent years listening to the opinions of others and the cravings of our flesh. How do we then set aside all these cares? We need to eat, work, and keep life running in our homes. Today, spend time asking the Lord how this 'setting aside' looks for you.

Wounded

The watchmen who go about the city found me. They struck me, they wounded me; the keepers of the walls took my veil and my mantle from me.

The Song of Songs 5:7

Before, we saw the watchmen of the city pointing the way for this wayward soul toward her bridegroom. Now we see they have struck and wounded her. Those who watch and guard the flock of the shepherd through prayer and supplication will often be the ones God uses to bring direction when we forsake Him. While instruction may be viewed as harsh, truth in love is often initially met with resistance and offense.

In some cases, we may seek out the comforting words of friends or trusted acquaintances, but rather than comfort, like Job, we are on the receiving end of harsh criticism and gossip which wounds us. This word 'wounding' literally describes a splitting of something.

Direction from the Lord will often be confirmed with witnesses, and our choices have two directions. Will this wounding cause us to split in a direction away from our bridegroom, or will it cause us to see we err in not following Him? While in our minds we feel sin is doing wrong the proper measure of sin is disobedience to the Lord. The bride reclined on her couch and found herself doing works rather than His will.

The law of God, and the works it required, was never given to save but to show men their own inability to live for the Father. It was only the sacrifice of Jesus that allowed our sin conscience to be cleansed rather than covered. Paul speaks often to the Galatians about the need for grace instead of works. We are told to take care and learn from the example of the Israelites that we not fall into sin and condemnation, but instead rely on the grace of the cross and its finished work.

This finished work is what Paul exemplifies and is why the watchmen have removed her veil. Paul chastises those who show and teach that the salvation of Christ is grace and afterwards favor is by works. The hearts of new and old believers must be alert to the influx of dead works and the outworking of the law. It is powerless in our lives, and in no way can it save or set free those with whom we are called to fellowship.

While we may feel misery in the state these watchmen leave us in, the question arises if we will still seek Him in a state of humiliation by the world's standards. Do we seek accolades and sweet words of those around us, or do we seek the sweet words of our bridegroom who hung as a thief before the world for us?

When Moses descended from Mt. Sinai, his face glowed with the glory of the Lord, and he was required to veil it so the people could look upon him. Why is it so vital that our faces be unveiled?

Read Galatians 3:5

For whom does God work miracles for?

Read 1 Peter 4:12-13

When trials come what are we called to do? What happens during these trials?

Prayer: O sweet and loving God, When I stay asleep too long, Oblivious to all your many blessings, Please wake me, And sing to me your joyful song. It is a song without noise or note. It is a song of love beyond words. —Mechthild of Magdeburg

Application: All of us have experienced tests and trials of faith, but as we walk by faith through them, patience and endurance are the fruits we bear. Think back on a recent test or trial of faith. How did this trial of faith build patience and endurance? Write your answer in your journal.

Sick with Love

I charge you, O daughters of Jerusalem, if you find my beloved, that you tell him that I am sick from love [simply sick to be with him].

The Song of Songs 5:8

How much will He ask of us? Often, we have turned this question and asked how much He has for us. While the Father gives us all things richly to enjoy, it is only the complete surrender that satisfies our soul. It should humble us that as sinners Christ saw us fit to die for. This truth should change our heart and make it cry out for holiness, for perfect love is selfless love.

While wounded, we could cry out in our desire for revenge or cry out at the injustice of our treatment, but here she begs the daughters to convey one thing, her simple love and desire for Him. The Apostle Paul tells us that it is great to be made humble and brought low for His sake. When we find our humility, it is shown by great power the workings of Christ in us.

The bride has called upon strange help. When we receive correction and admonishment from the spiritual authorities in our lives, we are faced with a choice. We can continue submitting our lives to leadership appointed by the Father, or we can turn our back and seek Him in the world exemplified by these daughters because of offense stemming from correction.

These Daughters don't know where the King of Kings may be found, nor do they have any answers that would spur her on toward Christ. The bride's sense of failure and humiliation from correction has caused her to stare at her heart and see lack. Her cry of love sickness is one of emptiness. Only her bridegroom will suffice.

Have there been instances where you received correction or instruction from believers that was hard to hear? Think back on that time and how you handled this situation. Did you react as the bride did here? Why?

Read 1 Timothy 5:20

When is rebuke called for in the body of Christ? Who should rebuke? Where should this be done? Why do you believe God has put this process in place?

Read Titus 1:12-14

What is the reason for this rebuke? What should come of it?

Read Hebrews 13:7 in the amplified

Who should we remember in prayer? What should we observe?

Prayer: I pray, Lord, that through the power of the Holy Spirit, You would help me to know You more. Each day, stir up my heart to seek Your presence and help in every situation, and help me grasp Your love and affection. In Jesus name, amen.

Activation: In John chapter 1, we read that Jesus is the Word and that He was with God in the very beginning. To know the Father more, we can seek Him in the Word. If you haven't committed to a Bible reading plan I encourage you to do so. This can simply be a plan to read a chapter a day from any book, or you can find reading plans on our Pinterest page. These plans will lead you through the Bible completely in just one year. Check it out at pinterest.com /dtmssm

A Written Epistle

What is your beloved more than another beloved; O you fairest among women [taunted the ladies]? What is your beloved more than another beloved, that you should give us such a charge?

The Song of Songs 5:9

O fairest among women? Even though wounded, they see the deep desire to find her bridegroom and the beauty of her pure love. Though they taunt, it is in a manner that they also wish to see who is this that one would sacrifice so much for?

Many would believe it is only the high points of our lives that speak of God and His goodness, but this is not so. How we speak and act under pressure and during our trials will impact many around us. Only those who have a relationship with the King of Kings can find joy and peace during such times. It is our personal relationship with God that distinguishes Christianity from all other faiths.

This trial of walking by faith and not by sight can be difficult. We don't always understand why there are delays in our prayers being answered, or the raise coming through, or the reconciliation of a friend, but in the midst of trials, when we cannot understand what God is doing, we simply trust His heart. This will speak to those around us. They will see that something within their own lives is missing, and we should be ready to share the wondrous love and peace of our bridegroom.

Consider the Daughter's question. How would you describe why Jesus is so much greater than any other?

Read Romans 5:3

What do these troubles produce in our hearts?

Read Romans 8:28

What is the promise of this verse?

Prayer: I thank You, Jesus, for a renewed heart and mind that can understand Your love in the midst of trials and uncertainty. I pray for heavenly focus, that my mind would immediately seek You when circumstances seem bleak. In Jesus name, amen.

Activation: Losing sight of the big picture is easy when we're being tossed about by circumstance and difficulty. The true big picture for believers is we have a promise and a hope in Christ. Take time today to ask the Lord how you can keep this big picture in front of you when things get difficult. Write what you hear in your journal.

Chief of Myriads

[She said] My beloved is fair and ruddy, the chief among ten thousand.

The Song of Songs 5:10

Once the bridegroom is far from her and the world is taunting her, asking how great He can be, we see our fair betrothed crying out he is dazzling! The bridegroom is many things to us- savior, love, friend, so many things that we could exclaim his greatness forever. All that the Lord has done and is doing for us causes our hearts to proclaim He is great, the chief among ten thousand.

This word ten thousand literally means a myriad. A group so large it can overwhelm and defy the senses. We see it first used in scripture in Leviticus 26:8 when the Lord is establishing His covenant with Israel. It was a promise that whoever went on the offensive against the enemy would always prevail, even when outnumbered by a myriad.

Our new and greater covenant grants us this victory, not for what we can do or accomplish, but what out bridegroom already finished for us. He is the chief that overtakes the enemy. His name is above all names, and He grants us the use of His name in every circumstance. He is white with purity and red with blood.

For the bride to have seen the Lord dazzling and brilliant, she would have seen the Lord glorified. When or how did the bride see the Lord?

Read Deuteronomy 33:2 and Habakkuk 3:3-4

Who was this coming from Sinai? What happened in the Earth when He appeared in glory?

Read 1 Samuel 16:12

What is the significance of this comparison between David and the bridegroom both being ruddy?

Read Luke 9:28-30

Who were the witnesses to the Lord's transfiguration? What was the Lord doing upon the mountain?

Prayer: I thank You and praise You, Lord, for Your goodness and mercy. Let my heart cry that You are dazzling. Let the truth of Your glory ever be on my lips and in my heart. In Jesus name, amen.

Application: Thinking of your walk with Christ, what are all the ways you would call Him dazzling? Write your thoughts in your journal.

King of Glory

His head is [as precious as] the finest gold; his locks are curly and bushy and black as a raven.

The Song of Songs 5:11

The betrothed is so enamored by her love for the Bridegroom, she begins to expound upon why He is dazzling. His head, she says, is as precious as gold. Not only is Christ the head of the church, we are told by Paul that as believers we too have the mind of Christ. It is for knowing and understanding His purposes and His heart. (1 Cor 2:16)

When we know and understand our purpose in Christ, it's easy to follow Him and lay aside our own desires. This bride begins to understand following Him is worth ridicule and seeking with her whole heart. This encounter with the Daughters of Jerusalem is an open door for proclaiming her Bridegroom's goodness and love. When we share His love for us and the world with others, it is our fulfillment of preaching to the world.

The raven sent from the ark by Noah did not return. It was a bird that devoured flesh of the dead. It was never to be eaten and was thought useless or worthless by Jews in history, but they too were preserved by Noah in the ark. A greater revelation comes when we study the ravens who fed Elijah in the wilderness.

1 Kings 17:1 "Elijah the Tishbite, of the temporary residents of Gilead, said to Ahab, As the Lord, the God of Israel, lives, before Whom I stand, there shall not be dew or rain these years but according to My word. And the word of the Lord came to him, saying, Go from here and turn east and hide yourself by the brook Cherith, east of the Jordan. You shall drink of the brook, and I have commanded the ravens to feed you there."

The ravens sent forth by Noah searched for land as the Earth dried up after the flood. Here we see they care for Elijah as the land of Gilead dries up by the word of the prophet.

Our Lord was teaching Elijah an important lesson about the worth of a thing. While many would say no good could come of a scavenger or an unclean thing, the Lord used the ravens to feed and serve Elijah during the drought. Elijah's attitude toward the wayward Israelites was similar. He viewed them as a backsliding ungodly people who were unworthy of God's grace. The truth is that all are unworthy of His grace, but it is not our worth in actions and deeds that moved the Father to send His Son for us. It was love.

While the ravens obeyed and the children of Israel didn't, Elijah learned he was not the only righteous man left in Israel. In fact, the Lord told him there were seven thousand. Rather than doubt the faith and obedience of those the world deems worthless, remember the Lord uses those same ones the world may reject.

Our raven-haired bridegroom was rejected by those in authority just as Elijah in authority had rejected those who he was called to speak to. Some view Jesus as a historical figure, others doubt His very existence, but to show His love for us, the Father sent a son. One who was obedient unto death, viewed as worthless by the world around Him, but who provides daily our bread of life.

The head of Christ is often adorned with a crown or diadem. How might the raven black hair mentioned by the bride be like a crown upon His head?

Read 1 Peter 2:7

Here Christ is called the Stone and Cornerstone. What is the significance of a cornerstone on a building?

Read Matthew 7:24-25

Who is the rock we build our faith upon? What can this faith withstand?

Read Colossians 2:10

In Christ, what do believers have? What does Jesus rule over?

Read 2 Corinthians 4:7

What precious treasure do we possess? Why do we have this treasure?

Prayer: Lord, open my eyes to see the world as You see it. Help me see Your image and fingerprint in every individual whether they have called upon Christ or have yet to enter Your kingdom. I pray that You would expand my capacity for love, mercy, and grace toward the unsaved, and I ask You use me to show Your truth toward them daily. In Jesus name, amen.

Activation: One of the hardest teachings to embrace is blessing those who curse us. When we view people through God's eyes, it's easier to see why He asks such a thing. Many are hurt and in turn hurt others. Take time today to think about those who have been mean to you or who have hurt you. Ask the Lord how you can pray for them today.

His Gaze

His eyes are like doves beside the water brooks, bathed in milk and fitly set.

The Song of Songs 5:12

Previously, it was the bridegroom that noted the eyes of a dove behind the veil of His betrothed. While those eyes were hidden, these eyes are prominently on display. To see someone, we must fix our eyes upon them, and to focus on someone, we must clearly see. Our bridegroom has eyes of a dove, a bird that searches out a foothold, a firm footing to rest upon. Are His eyes turned to us?

However strange the change in comparisons may seem, from raven to dove, it is an important shift in this bride describing her bridegroom. While many would consider laying down a life to follow Him a terrible sacrifice, she extols He is truly a sacrifice worthy of praise. Jesus laid aside His deity to rescue. It is a truth that will open the hardest hearts.

In the book of Leviticus, we are told that bathing is necessary for priestly functions, and in 1 Peter 2:2, we are told to crave the pure spiritual milk of the word. This allegory is exemplified in Ephesians 5:25-27 where we are told Christ cleansed us by washing us with the Word. Here all examples of Christ come together to describe His priestly ministry and function. Those dove eyes are bathed in the milk of the Word which cleanses those, whom His eyes find their rest.

While we are kings and priests in the kingdom, we must seek the One who brought us into relationship with Himself. It is when we read the word prayerfully, praying its truths over ourselves and others, that we open our spiritual eyes to see others and Jesus sees them.

Why do we find it difficult to pray for those who hurt us? Is it easier for you to pray for strangers or people you know?

Read Psalm 34:15

Who does the Lord gaze upon? What does the Holy Spirit do in us that's similar to having the gaze of the Lord upon us?

Read Psalm 36:7-9

Where do we rest? What do we drink? Where does this water come from?

Read Revelation 22:1

Where does the water of life originate? What does it feed?

Prayer: Lord, You are dazzling and full of resurrection life. Let my life be wholly dedicated to You. Come and live through my words, my hands, my feet. Let this life be resurrected in service to You as no other will satisfy me. In Jesus name, amen.

Application: Thinking of a life lived in full service, are there areas of your life that need to be given to Christ? Write your thoughts in your journal.

His Words

His cheeks are like a bed of spices or balsam, like banks of sweet herbs yielding fragrance. His lips are like blood red anemones or lilies distilling liquid [sweet-scented] myrrh.

The Song of Songs 5:13

Isaiah tells us the spotless Lamb offered his cheeks to those who scorned Him so they would pluck out His beard (Isaiah 50:6). It was for the church that He did not hide His face in shame, but reveled in the scorn the enemy would bring his way. It was His offering to us and it was sweet as the herbs that grow near the waters.

The word that issues from the mouth of the Lord does not return void nor does it ever change. We can believe and trust His gospel is good news. In Proverbs 9, Solomon compares this to wisdom which flows from the mouth of the righteous and is acceptable to Him. These lips that drop myrrh share the wisdom that is the grace of His death and suffering.

Read Luke 4:22

Why did the teachers marvel at the words of Jesus?

Matthew 27:29-31

In what way did Jesus show submission and humility?

Philippians 2:5-8

What did Jesus lay aside? Why did He do this? What did God do in response?

Read 1 Kings 7:19

What was decorated with lilies in the temple?

Prayer: Thank You, Lord, for the Good News. I pray that every believer is empowered by Your Spirit to share its truth in boldness. I pray that You would open doors for the Word to go forth in every place. Let every opposing voice be silent and truth to reign. In Jesus name, amen.

Activation: Ask the Lord if there is a person you can share the Good News with today. Pray for boldness and empowerment to share the truth of the Gospel. Be sure to write down all these encounters in your journal. You can share them with us too! @Discipleshiptr1 on twitter

His Hands

His hands are like rods of gold set with [nails of] beryl or topaz. His body is a figure of bright ivory overlaid with [veins of] sapphires.

The Song of Songs 5:14

These divine hands are eternal and are set with beryl. The breastplate of the High Priest contained twelve stones each representing a tribe of Israel (Ex. 28:21). The stones were engraved with a tribe's name in their order of birth. The tenth tribe was Zebulon, which means, an abode which glorifies its occupant. It is also a stone within the foundation of the Heavenly Jerusalem described in Revelation chapter 21.

The word beryl in Hebrew is תרשיש Tarshish, the place where Jonah tried to flee. His attempts to flee the call of God are far more relatable to the believer than we care to admit. Often, we see those in the world, living in sin, and have no care for their salvation. The Lord speaks a powerful message in this passage. He formed all men with His hands, and those same hands that bore the nail holes did so for all. It is not for us to deny him His people.

160

The word Tarshish comes from several roots; each when combined add an interesting and poignant look at the hands of this bridegroom she so desperately desires to share. The noun שׁשׁ *shesh* means six and also alabaster and the other root תּוֹר *tor* means dove. These divine hands that may seem like rods are really more like those alabaster lilies growing in the valley adorned with the sweetness of the Holy Spirit.

In 1 Corinthians 12, Paul tells the members of the church they are indeed the Body of Christ and He is the head. When we act on the will of the Father, we bring this good news of salvation and are His hands and feet in the Earth. We have been washed white and are clothed in righteousness, but we are inlaid with sapphire.

Why is the bride telling the Daughters of Jerusalem about the hands of the bridegroom? Why is it significant to share details about the Author of our faith?

Psalm 110:1

Who sits at God's right hand? What is the significance of this position?

Habakkuk 3:3-4

Where does the Lord come from? How does the earth respond to the Lord? Where is the Lord's power?

Read Revelation 21:3

What is the promise of this verse? How does this promise correlate to the Zebulon beryl stone?

Prayer: Lord, I pray for a humble heart, one that leans entirely on Your redemptive work. As You lead and guide me, let Your goodness, grace, and love be fully visible. In Jesus name, amen.

Activation: List the tribes of Israel according to their birth. Look up the names of each and write down their meaning. Meditate on the fullness of what the Lord was saying to the people of Israel every time they looked upon the high priest.

His Strength

His legs are like strong and steady pillars of marble set upon bases of fine gold. His appearance is like Lebanon, excellent, stately, and majestic as the cedars.

The Song of Songs 5:15

Pillars are used to hold something upright. It is through Christ that we are found upright in the Father's sight. It was not by our works, but by our faith in Him that we are saved and walk in righteousness. The word translated marble is often translated 'fine linen' in other verses of scripture. The saints of God are clothed in this fine linen of righteousness and right standing with the Father, which is based on the incorruptible foundation of Christ's redemption.

The first use of this word is found in Genesis 41 when Pharaoh gave Joseph his signet ring and clothed him in fine linen. This sign of authority and headship over Egypt is symbolic of our bridegroom's rule and reign over the world. The law itself could not save, but we needed our kinsman redeemer who lived as one of us to set us free. He is eternal but is as natural as the cedars living as the last Adam. In this human body, Jesus came to fulfill all the law and do so without sin so that humanity would be redeemed.

The personal nature and humanity of our Savior is God's design and gentle call to relationship. Adherence to rules and regulations, as demonstrated by the Israelites, was never the design of the Father. This is so unlike the empty promises of other faiths. Our assurance of faith is that Christ our Redeemer is truly the lover of our souls.

How would you describe the relationship you have with Christ your bridegroom? Why is the personal nature of this relationship significant to you?

Read Genesis 35:8-15

What did this pillar of stone represent? What offering was made here?

Read Psalm 92:12

Who is likened to the palm tree and cedar in this verse?

Read Romans 8:29-30

Who are believers being molded into? How does this occur?

Read Romans 5:15-21

List all the sins and their consequence of Adam's fall. Compare this to the grace and favor Christ provided for each. Explain why salvation being a free gift is significant compared to other religions. Why do you believe the bride emphasized this point to the Daughters of Jerusalem?

Prayer: Jesus, I thank You and Praise You for the gift of righteousness. I pray that my heart and mind stay focused on this gift that cannot be earned, but is available to all. Let my words speak this truth that You are the righteous one. In Jesus name, amen.

Activation: Take time today to focus on rest and restoration.

My Beloved, My Friend

His voice and speech are exceedingly sweet; yes, he is altogether lovely [the whole of him delights and is precious].This is my beloved, and this is my friend, O daughters of Jerusalem!

The Song of Songs 5:16

Everything our bridegroom says and does is for our benefit. It should be impossible for believers to keep His glory and majesty shut away inside us. We should praise Him loudly and with zeal to those who may not know His grace. This is our beloved O Daughters of Jerusalem! Do you wish to know Him as beloved too? All these joys, all this peace, has been made available to those who believe. Who would not answer?

In the previous verses, the bride has extolled the excellence of the bridegroom. While we may say the virtues of our bridegroom are without number, we see the bride-to-be shows us nine particular virtues. One might ask why only nine, or why these nine in particular? His head is gold, His locks black as a raven, His eyes like doves, Cheeks a bed of spices, lips dripping with myrrh, hands of gold set with beryl, abdomen of ivory set with sapphire, legs pillars of alabaster, mouth full of sweetness.

The Hebrew number nine carries with it the implications of fruitfulness and new life. We read of the nine Gifts of the Sprit found in those who call upon the Lord and work to accomplish His will. The outworking of the Gifts of the Spirit in our lives helps show the many facets of the Father and His desire for the hearts of His children. His wisdom is spoken to help guide us.

A word of knowledge for insight, A gift of faith to encourage when things appear hopeless, and gifts of healing to draw those in need to the love of the Father. Miracles to show the desire of our Father to set us free from the enemy's hold, and Prophecy to encourage and give witness to those things the Father has shown us. Discernment of spirits to help as watchmen on the walls of the church keeping the enemy from within, and Tongues to pray when we don't know how. Interpretation of tongues to share those hidden truths with the body of Christ.

In Galatians 5, we see there are also nine different Fruits of the Spirit. It is the Spirit that reveals to us the truth of our newness in Christ. It is also the spirit that works regeneration within us. This new life and new truth produce fruitfulness in us with outworkings of love, joy, peace, patience, kindness, benevolence, faithfulness, gentleness, and self-control.

Jesus sent us the Holy Spirit after He went away because it was necessary for the growth of each believer and the growth of the church. When He lived among us, Jesus could only reach a limited number of people with healing and the truth of the Gospel. Now that the Holy Spirit indwells every believer, we can reach the whole earth and fill it with His glory.

The Holy Spirit is described as a dove so it's important we understand a dove's characteristics so we may glean knowledge and insight as to why this analogy is made. The wings of a dove each have nine primary feathers. It's necessary for proper flight for these feathers to be in balance and properly utilized. For the Holy Spirit to be fully functional and properly understood, we must embrace the balance it brings. Those Fruits of the Spirit are the inner workings to help develop us into disciples of Christ, and the Gifts of the Spirit are for the effectual working of our discipleship.

This precious gift of the Holy Spirit that leads, guides, and helps grow us, is why the bride exclaims His words are sweet. At one time, we all sought inner peace and wholeness through the world, but our bridegroom is personal, and through the Holy Spirit, His sweetness is revealed directly to our hearts.

What words do you most often use to describe Jesus? Have you called Him beloved or friend?

Read Haggai 2:4

Who is the desire of all nations? How do the nations learn of Him?

Read 2 Corinthians 5:19-20

What has been committed to the righteous? What are believers now called? Describe the role of ambassador.

Read Matthew 5:13-16

How does the Lord describe His followers? What has the bride done for the Daughters of Jerusalem? Who were the brides in your life? How did they share Christ with you? What was your response?

Prayer: Father, I thank You for sending the Holy Spirit to equip and enable me to share the gospel with signs, wonders, and miracles. I pray that You would fill me up to overflowing and begin to grow the Gifts of the Spirit in me. In Jesus name, amen.

Activation: Take time today to ask the Lord what gifts of the Spirit you need growth in. Write down what you hear in your journal and make an effort to ask the Father how you can grow in that gift.

CHAPTER 6

The Bride of Christ Unveiled

A Hungry Heart

Where has your beloved gone, O you fairest among women? Where is your beloved hiding himself? For we would seek him with you.

The Song of Songs 6:1

In this world where the hearts of men fail them out of fear and the lies of the enemy bombard us daily, it can overwhelm us to see love, compassion, and freedom. This love of our bridegroom will win the hearts of many if we are ready to share it. "Where is He? We need to find Him too!" they cried.

Do we preach the love, perfection, and grace of His countenance with such fervor that those who hear it are drawn to Him? Once we set aside all and follow Him with abandon, we become a great witness to the world around us. It is when they see the virtues of the bridegroom on display in us that they too begin to seek Him with joy.

What feel knowing that though He abides in us, He is with the Father? Do we still seek Him in others or do we now lead them to Him just as we were once led? Jesus now sits at the Father's right hand. He makes intersession for us as we live this life, and He silences the accuser of our souls in the courts of Heaven so that nothing might hinder us as we live for Him.

What was your first response to the witness of Christ? What drew you about their testimony or countenance?

Read John 12:25-26

How has this bride despised or forsaken her life? What was the result?

Read Acts 1:8

What empowers believers to be a witness for the Lord? Why do we need the Holy Spirit to share the Good News?

Prayer: Lord, I thank You for the precious gift of Your Son. I pray now for boldness to proclaim the truth of the gospel wherever You call me to go. Let my mouth be filled with the words You have to share, and let my life proclaim Your mercy and goodness. In Jesus name, amen.

Application: Have you ever been a part of organized evangelism and outreach? Step out today and find an outreach near you where you can join with other believers and share the Good News of Jesus Christ. Check out www.timetorevive.com or www.billygraham.org

Leading Others to Him

[She replied] My beloved has gone down to his garden, to the beds of spices, to feed in the gardens and to gather lilies.

The Song of Songs 6:2

Where is He? Remembering His faithfulness, the bride again follows the path her bridegroom laid out for her. She wasted so much time trying in her own wisdom and strength to find Him only to remember He is always with her, and He is always with His followers.

It is never our place to hold our bridegroom in one place, but we must understand the heart of the King for His people. The garden of our heart belongs to Him, but why would this be? It's not only where we see fruitfulness, but also where we perceive the will of the Father.

The Garden of Eden where Adam walked with God was the Father's will. Being made in His image and likeness is where we see the desire that man know Him personally and without hindrance. The Garden of Gethsemane is where we see the heart of Jesus.

His agony in the garden may be similar to the temptation in the wilderness, but its effects on His soul were much greater. Here our Lord sweat great drops of blood as His soul poured out to the Father. While the first Adam fell, our Lord, the second Adam, redeemed us in this garden and restored us to relationship by submitting Himself to the perfect will of God.

The witnesses of this great trial were the three closest to His heart. Now He inhabits the hearts of all believers. These are the lilies. Those who are white as snow by His shed blood on the cross. The garden was a surrendering of wills, Jesus to the will of the Father, just as our will must surrender in the garden Jesus now enjoys in our hearts.

Spend time thinking about the scene at Gethsemane and compare this to the scene at the tree in the Garden of Eden. What was the heart motive of our Lord? What was the motive of Adam?

Read Psalm 22:8

Why does the Lord rescue and save? What does the word 'delight' mean?

Read Romans 10:8-9 and Deuteronomy 30:14

Compare these verses and note their differences. Describe how they differ and what that means for believers today.

Prayer: Jesus, I thank You for enduring the cross. I praise Your name for salvation and restoration and believing my life was worth it. Come and enjoy the garden of my heart. All I am is Yours. Thank You for the Holy Spirit who reveals the Word and the will of the Father. In Jesus name, amen.

Activation: Take time this week to visit a garden or park. Spend time reading the word and praying while you're there. This is an excellent time to ask the Lord for revelation about what He enjoys in your heart. Write your thoughts and feelings in your journal.

Beloved

I am my beloveds and my beloved is mine! He feeds among the lilies.

The Song of Songs 6:3

As she shakes off hindrances to following her bridegroom as a disciple, her soul shouts I am my beloved's. No greater joy can be found in this life than to know who inhabits our heart. We were created by the Father for Him, and it is our deepest desire to be in covenant with Him. Everyone is fully capable to do His will and good pleasure as we were created by Him and for His purpose. It is important to see that while she still calls her bridegroom her own, she knows it's only because she is first His.

The lilies where He delights are others who have joined themselves to Him. The Word tells us that He never leaves us, nor does he forsake us, and though there may be times when it seems His presence is hidden, we simply don't find Him where we search. It is wise then to understand the bridegroom delights in all who follow Him and is always with them.

What is the significance of this statement being reversed, i.e. mine/His to His/mine?

Read Isaiah 43:7

What are believers created for? What do you believe glorifies the Father?

Read 1 John 5:10-12

What do believers in Christ have? How is that testimony and life shown in this verse?

Prayer: I lift my heart to You today, Lord. I invite You to come in and search me. If You find anything that has taken Your place help me realign it so You would be first in my life. Remind me again of the day I made You Lord of my life, and help me to focus on everything You have done in me since. In Jesus name, amen.

Activation: Take time today to read through your journal. It's good to remind ourselves of all the awesome things the Lord has done in our lives. If you have any encounters to add write it down.

Beautiful Inheritance

[He said] You are as beautiful as Tirzah, my love, and as comely as Jerusalem, as terrible as a bannered host!

The Song of Songs 6:4

The Canaanite city of Tirzah was named for the daughter of Zelophehad. Tirzah and her four sisters challenged the Law of Moses with their entreaty before entering the promised land. Her Father had no sons and died in the wilderness. It was their heart that his name not die out; they asked for an inheritance among their uncles. The Lord responded that they should receive a fair share of the land.

It is significant that this woman be mentioned by the bridegroom. It was the first instance in the Word that a woman inherited property from her Father. There is an inheritance through Jesus for the Body of Christ, and He says to her, "Ask of me what is rightfully yours!" (Ephesians 1:11)

This inheritance is as comely as the holy city of Jerusalem. While we may desire to see its temple or enter its courts, we live now with a better covenant. One that makes room for the new temple found in our hearts. We are made kings and priests of the Lord, but we are also soldiers in his army. The enemy should tremble at the thought of what our words can do and the armies of the Lord they can slay.

There is again a gentle reminder to this comparison. The city of Tirzah was home to the kings of the Northern Kingdom. While the city itself was lovely to behold, the hearts of the people strayed from the will of the Father. They forsook the temple sacrifices in Jerusalem and worshiped God in their own way and by their own means. We have an inheritance through Christ and no longer sacrifice upon altars, but our hearts should yearn for the leading of the Holy Spirit to follow the Father's will.

This banner proclaims the army is the Lord's. The Holiness of Christ appears terrible for it illuminates the sin and need of salvation in the hearts of those who behold it. All believers walk in righteousness, but this holiness is a separate choice. We can choose to obey the Lord and do His will, or we can neglect the sanctified life of a disciple. This bride has finally understood that fellowship is only part of this life with Him.

Read Ephesians 5:21-32

Explain in your own words the meaning of these verses concerning Christ and the Church.

Read Revelation 21:2

What is the bride likened to? What attributes does the Bride of Christ carry that would liken her to the New Jerusalem?

Read 2 Corinthians 3:18

If righteousness is given when we declare Jesus Christ our Lord, what is the process being described in this verse?

Read Psalm 60:4

What does the Lord give? Why? What is this truth?

Prayer: I praise You, Jesus, for the promise of an inheritance in Your name. I thank you for restoring me to righteousness and sharing Your victory that I would be victorious. Help me to continue in the will of the Father and not stray to do my own will. In Jesus name, amen.

Activation: Praise and worship isn't just for church! Take time today to praise the Lord with a melody. Find your favorite praise and worship music and make it a special time between you and the Lord.

Overcoming Love

Turn away your eyes from me, for they have overcome me! Your hair is like a flock of goats trailing down from Mount Gilead.

The Song of Songs 6:5

Before, the bridegroom noted she had the eyes of a dove behind her veil and she asked him to turn away from her darkness. Now he is overcome. While the bridegroom praises her again for her hair, he does not note the eyes behind her veil. Paul writes in Corinthians that we must behold the Lord without a covering so we may truly be transformed into His image.

As we continually behold Jesus, a desire to grow in relationship with Him will develop. As this change within us takes place, the broken pieces that were fallen man are made whole again. It is only the work of the Holy Spirit within us that can change our heart and our habits. The Holy Spirit is called the revealer of Christ; it is He who removes this veil from our eyes. Now we behold Him and can return this expression of overwhelming love.

The Father clearly sees the hearts of men and perceives their motives. When this bride beholds her bridegroom, her love for Him is overwhelming. This is because it is a selfless love. One which desires the presence of the bridegroom more than it desires His provision.

In John 14, the Lord speaks to the disciples concerning the coming of the Holy Spirit. He tells them that after the Comforter comes, those who continue on in obedience to the Word and Spirit are those who truly love Him. They are those who seek the person of Christ and behold Him. How can we now behold Christ?

As we take care to read the Word we are beholding Jesus. Take Him in daily and behold the glory of the One who set us free. We are daily covering ourselves like the goats of Gilead covered the mountain.

How would you invite the presence of the bridegroom into your life in a meaningful way?

Read Hebrews 4:12

How is the Word alive? What does it do inside those who read it?

Read Exodus 33:13

What did Moses request from the Lord? What was the answer?

Prayer: Father, I pray You make me more like Jesus. Take my heart, change what needs to be changed, and open my eyes to see the world how You see it. Teach me to hold my words if they don't edify. Help me by the Holy Spirit to develop the Fruits of the Spirit that my life would be a living testimony of Your goodness. In Jesus name, amen.

Application: Ask the Lord today if there are any Fruits of the Spirit you need to mature or grow in. Ask Him for the Holy Spirit to help you. Write down all you hear in your journal.

Praises of the Bridegroom

Your teeth are like a flock of ewes coming from their washing, of which all are in pairs,
and not one of them is missing.

The Song of Songs 6:6

These sheep are not described as shorn as they were before. Newly shorn ewes are a sign of springtime and lambing. This move away from spring would be a progression of seasons in the land and also a sign of progression in the lives of believers. They are also not called alike; He notes that they are in pairs.

The Lord sent out his disciples in pairs to share the good news that the kingdom of heaven was at hand. As a sign of His authority and the truthfulness of his Word, signs, and wonders followed those who answered this call and went forth. We are also called to go forth and lead others to Jesus with the help of others in the body. The birth of the church in the upper room was preceded by prayer and worship in unity.

As we incorporate more and more of the Word into our hearts, we are changed and see the church as a unified body striving toward the Good News being shared. In John 6, we see Jesus called the bread of life, which we ingest and meditate on daily. This daily meditation and reading of the word of life washes us clean and progresses us toward being more like Him.

How does maturity lead to unity within a group of believers? Why is unity in the body so vital to fulfilling the call?

Read Ephesians 5:26

Why must we be washed daily? How do you believe the Word cleanses us?

Read Mark 6:7

What are believers called? Why did Jesus send them in pairs?

Read Ephesians 4:12-14

Why are the saints equipped? What does this lead to? What are we then?

Prayer: Lord, I praise You for never giving up on me. Every time I fall short, Your love and grace is all-sufficient. I pray that by Your spirit You would help me know and understand the depth of Your provision and abundant grace. Help me grow from glory to glory in the knowledge of Christ so that I would be equipped to do every good work. In Jesus name, amen.

Activation: We all have moments in life when we feel overwhelmed. But God is always with us and is always for us. Spend time today thinking back on any times God has shown up in a mighty way when you've felt like giving up. Write the story down in your journal. Remember that every instance of His miraculous works is a testimony to share with others. Be ready for who you'll share it with.

Temples of Truth

Your cheeks are like halves of a pomegranate behind your veil.

The Song of Songs 6:7

Her cheeks are like the pomegranate. One does not partake of a pomegranate without great thought and care. The many seeds the fruit contains are hard and bitter, each surrounded by blood-red nectar. In chapter 4, the Lord mentioned the pomegranate along with her scarlet mouth, but nothing of her lips is mentioned here.

How does her mouth change throughout these passages? We see the bride uses her words to share the love of Christ with others and allows herself to be a mouthpiece for the Kingdom's purpose. Those lips of scarlet are now fruitful and speak of even greater things than His blood. They speak of resurrection life and truth and continually sow the seed of God's Word into the hearts of men.

In Luke chapter 8, we see Jesus telling us the parable of the sower. As the farmer scattered his seed, it all fell on different types of ground. Hard ground that was trampled underfoot which the birds ate. How often do we see people so hardened by life they reject any good news? Then some seed fell on rocky soil only to wither when heat and trials befell it. Again, how often do we see people receive the truth only to deny it when trials come?

Then there is the seed which gets scattered among the thorns. It sprouts and grows, but the cares of life and the worries of our mind choke out the possibility of producing fruit. Finally, there is the good soil. A heart which is not only receptive to the truth when it comes but grows and tends the Word of Truth so it produces fruits that others may glean. This is the heart of the bride. Her heart is a delightful garden which feeds and nourishes others by planting and helping tend this truth.

How might you help prepare or tend the heart of another person?

Read Acts 14:21-22

What was the purpose of the Apostle's teaching? Why did they teach?

Read 1 Corinthians 3:6-8

What might be the differences between this planting and watering? Who causes the growth? What happens to those who plant or water?

Prayer: Thank You, Lord, that you open doors that no man can shut. I pray now for opportunities to share the gospel of Christ with people who need You. Let my mouth be ready and my heart inclined to hear what You say. I pray that hearts will be ready to hear the truth and minds will be clear. Let Your name be glorified in all I do. In Jesus name, amen.

Activation: Listen intently today to the Holy Spirit and be ready to share with someone as the Lord leads. This may be simply praying for someone, sharing part of your testimony, or leading them in a prayer of salvation. God uses all believers at different times and in different places.

Steps to Intimacy

There are sixty queens and eighty concubines, and virgins without number;

The Song of Songs 6:8

A queen is one who wears a crown and shares a throne. It's a political position. While queens may enjoy the privilege of ruling, they do not cherish nor do they share the king's heart. They are not the subject of his thoughts, and the heart of the King is wounded by their indifference.

Concubines are those believers who have begun experiencing the joy of fellowship and intimacy with the Lord. They may be believers who wish to have a superficial relationship with the King. They simply the objects and trinkets he is able to provide, but they don't care to toil with kingdom works. It is possible to enjoy brief glimpses of the king while a concubine, but it was only at the king's desire and leisure that they were called upon.

Virgins without number, they have been washed by the blood and saved by grace, but they have no fellowship with their Lord. They are the ones who do not pursue Him, nor do they follow his commands. They are happy and content to be free of the fiery pit, but to do the work of the kingdom or approach the Father through prayer is beyond their desire.

Have you experienced these stages of relationship with Jesus? What motivated you to pursue Him further?

Read John 18:37

What is the promise of this verse? What ways do we hear and know the truth?

Revelation 2:26

What is the promise given to those who obey the commands of the Lord? Why do we obey the leading of the Holy Spirit?

Read John 14:23

How do we know and keep the commands of the Lord?

Prayer: Lord, I love You. Not for the things You give me, but because You are good, kind, gentle, loving, merciful, and beautiful. Help me continue to seek to know You even more. I pray that the distractions keeping me from spending time in Your presence would fade away. Lord, change my heart to want You more. In Jesus name, amen.

Activation: There may come a time when we share a testimony or an encouraging word with someone who is already a believer. Spend some time today asking the Lord how you might be used to encourage someone.

The Dove

But my dove, my undefiled and perfect one, stands alone [above them all]; she is the only one of her mother, she is the choice one of her who bore her. The daughters saw her and called her blessed and happy, yes, the queens and the concubines, and they praised her.

The Song of Songs 6:9

We must see ourselves as doves, surrendered to the will of the Father and accomplishing those things we have been called to do. How do we hear the will of the Father? We must listen to the voice of the Holy Spirit, the dove. The wings of a dove each have nine primary feathers, and to be balanced in our walk with the Holy Spirit we must grow in understanding of all its workings.

The nine Gifts of the Spirit and nine Fruits of the Spirit all work in harmony to help us follow Him. These nine Gifts of the Spirit have three main workings. Three are gifts of knowing (a word of wisdom, a word of knowledge, a word of prophecy), three gifts of doing (working of miracles, a gift of faith, a gift of healing), and three gifts of speaking (discernment of spirits, gift of tongues, gift of interpretation) (1 Corinthians 12). These gifts are manifestations of the Holy Spirit for the benefit of and service to others.

The Fruits of the Spirit are those things that are being done inside us by the Holy Spirit to show the Father character to others. These fruits of love, goodness, faithfulness, gentleness, self-control, patience, kindness, peace, and joy are enjoyed by others when believers walk in their expression. They are not for their own personal benefit until they have been sown into their hearts by the same Spirit.

Why do they praise the dove? Because she is the one who sits above all the others. It is His perfect dove who not only understands her place in the king's heart, but also her place within the kingdom. As the bride of Christ arises to her place as the living hands and feet of the Lord, all who hunger and thirst for the God of creation will see His character in her.

Do you feel there is balance in your understanding of the Holy Spirit? Do you feel there is balance in your use of the gifts and fruits of the Spirit?

Read Psalm 92:14

What is the promise of this verse? What are believers rich in?

Read Ephesians 5:9

How does Paul describe the Fruits of the Spirit in this verse?

1 Peter 4:10

How are the Gifts of the Spirit to be used for the body?

Prayer: Lord, I pray now that the Holy Spirit would lead and guide me in all things. Let my heart be sensitive to all He says. I pray that the Holy Spirit would develop in me all the fruits and gifts that I would be an effective witness for the kingdom. In Jesus name, amen.

Application: Are there any Gifts of the Spirit that you have not walked in while ministering to others? Ask the Lord today for boldness and an opportunity to do so. Make sure you write down your encounter in your journal.

Showing His Countenance

[The ladies asked] Who is this that looks forth like the dawn, fair as the moon, clear and pure as the sun, and terrible as a bannered host?

The Song of Songs 6:10

The fruits and gifts of the Spirit working in us and through us will be noticed by others. Often, it is those who slowly grow in relationship with Him that are suddenly found front and center of his kingdom work. They compare this lovely bride to the moon who gives a gentle glow and peaceful countenance to those around her.

This light of the moon is a reflection of the sun. It is as a mirror we behold our Lord and through which transformed into His image, which is shown to all nations. As we are transformed in the true knowledge of the Lord, we act as His representatives and show the wonderful truth that all are welcome in the kingdom.

The enemy would see us as a host holding a banner. We have at our disposal the angels to go forth and make the paths we walk straight. The banners of armies proudly declared who they represented and who they fought for. We are the army of the Lord and our weapons are mighty.

Many believers today don't understand that Satan never ceased in his attempts to steal, kill, and destroy them. He causes confusion, church divisions, anger, bitterness, and resentment all on a daily basis. Many are tossed about by circumstances in life they feel are out of their control, or feel subject to broken relationships that seem irreparable.

The Word would never tell us to do what was impossible. It states that all things are possible to him who believes. Do we trust in the Lord enough to arm ourselves with His armor that we may stand before the enemy and never be defeated? Do we rely on His victory that makes us victorious in His name?

Read Ephesians 6:11

What must be put on to remain steadfast in the Word?

Read 1 Peter 2:9

How does the Lord see those in Christ? What are we called to do?

Read Psalm 89:36-37

Describe the relationship between Christ and believers shown in these verses.

Prayer: Father, I thank You for the gift of Your Son. I pray that as I grow closer to Christ, more of His life would reflect in me. Let this reflection be of the living Christ who overcame and set all the captives free. I praise You, Lord, for Your victory over sin and death. Come and continue to work in me. In Jesus name, amen.

Application: Sit before the Lord today with your journal open, and ask Him to reveal to you all the ways He sees you reflecting Christ. Write down all you hear.

Mentorship

I went down into the nut orchard to look at the green plants of the valley, to see whether the grapevine had budded and the pomegranates were in flower.

The Song of Songs 6:11

We see another parallel in this verse. Before the bride had enjoyed the shade of the trees offered to her. Now we see she begins to look for the growth and fruitfulness in others. The orchard is where we see what is progressing in our lives. Have we sown freely to others? Are those truths of God's Word growing in other people's lives? Eventually, we will be the mature believers who help to mature and grow others.

Discipleship is a common theme throughout the Word of God. From Jesus and the twelve to Paul and the churches in Asia, spiritual guidance and mentorship have helped shape the lives of countless believers. The Apostle Paul writes 'And let us consider how we may spur one another on toward love and good deeds,' (Hebrews 10:24).

Walking in love and doing good deeds are contrary to our flesh and its desires, and to have accountability and support within the body is crucial to overcoming natural thoughts and actions. The bride didn't allow herself to wallow in the praises of others. She immediately went to work inspecting the growth and life of those she was mentor over. The humility of heart is a sure sign of maturity and readiness to disciple others.

Do you have a Christian believer you regularly ask questions and gain wisdom from? How did this relationship form?

Read 1 Corinthians 2:6

Why is maturity in Christ vital to the growth of the church?

Read Matthew 16:24

What must be laid aside? Why is this necessary? Who do we follow? What does it cost?

Prayer: Father, help me mentor new believers for your glory. Let my heart toward these precious souls be soft with understanding and patience, and let my words be full of truth and love. I pray that every distraction of the enemy be silenced in Jesus' name. I pray for their ears to hear the truth and eyes to see Your grace. I pray for wisdom in leading and guiding through the Holy Spirit in Jesus name, amen.

Activation: Have you found yourself sharing the truths of the Word with the same people? Likely these relationships are the very ones God has called you to mentor. Ask the Lord what this should look like. Should you meet for study and sharing of hearts? Should you call each other on a regular basis and share struggles and triumphs? Mentorship takes shape between individuals with God as the head and every one looks slightly different.

Leadership

Before I was aware [of what was happening], my desire [to roam about] had brought me into the area of the princes of my people [the king's retinue].

The Song of Songs 6:12

Her deepest praises of the bridegroom have led others to question where such a great one could be. After praising Him, the bride understands He is so perfect He would never leave her. She shouts that she is His and in doing so begins to lead others to Him. She is praised for being a great witness and for having the same mind and will as the Father.

We are all called to be kings and priests of the kingdom. It is in understanding this that we are blessed to know him. Our growth leads us to greater maturity which does draw others, especially those who are new in this life. As our lives progress further into Him, we help

186

oversee the growth of others and teach by example. It is what Paul tells us in Philippians chapter 3. As we grow to be more like Christ in our minds and actions, we strive toward that calling He has for us.

This verse is the last of chapter 6 in the Hebrew book, as though this was the final thought tying the previous verses together. It was in her mind to view the growth in others, but before she could comprehend what changed, she was placed upon a chariot. Not as the horse pulling and straining under the bridle, but as the driver, the one who leads the charge of an army. One might say that growth in the kingdom of God comes with a fight.

This life in Christ is a fight. It is a fight to overcome the lies and deceptions of the enemy. It is a fight to believe that we are loved, cherished, and desired by the King. It is a fight to say we are content no matter what the circumstances may be or the obstacle we may face. Be ready always to fight for those things the bridegroom says are ours. The truth is they are ours, and if Satan can't deceive you, he cannot defeat you.

How might it be a fight against the enemy to disciple and lead others?

Read 1 Timothy 6:12

Why do you believe we must fight to lay hold of eternal 'life' if we are already saved by faith? What 'life' are you laying hold of? Hint. Look up this word *Zoe* in the Strong's or Thayer's Greek Lexicon.

Read Philippians 3:13-17

What is Paul's goal or aspiration? Why does he keep moving forward? Who has this mindset? For those who are not focused on the prize what should they do? Under what authority does Paul give this instruction?

Prayer: Jesus, I praise You that through Your victory I am victorious. In Your name I can overcome all lies, schemes, and accusations of the enemy, and through You I can fight the good fight of faith. I believe I have authority in Your name, so I command Satan to cease his attacks now in Jesus name. Amen.

Activation: In Ephesians, Paul talks about putting on the whole armor of God. We've studied the various pieces of armor mentioned and how they are applied, but the question remains; do we apply this armor every day as defense against attack? As followers of Christ, we often forget that the enemy sees us as threats to his kingdom and we neglect to arm ourselves daily. Make an effort today and this whole week to put on that armor daily. Don't forget the sword of the Spirit which is the Word of God.

Victory Dance

[I began to flee, but they called to me] Return, return, O Shulammite; return, return, that we may look upon you! [I replied] What is there for you to see in the [poor little] Shulammite? [And they answered] As upon a dance before two armies or a dance of Mahanaim.

The Song of Songs 6:13 or The Song of Songs 7:1

As our Lord reveals to us more and more the truth of who we are in Christ, we can accept His praises as truth or run from them. Here we see she fled from the knowledge that she is an overcomer and a leader in the army of God. Whether it is unbelief or a heart attitude that she is not worthy, the reason does not matter. We are all called according to His will and purpose, and we must take up this cross of will daily.

It is the first instance in this book, we see the bride referred to as Shulamite. Some would argue it means she is from Shulam, a city in the Jezreel valley south of Galilee near the foot of Mount Moriah. To view this woman as simply 'from Shulam', one would miss the most important reason for this nickname.

The word Shula stems from the word Shalem, coincidentally where Solomon's name also stems from. This root word Shalem many translate as peace or wholeness, but its meaning runs far deeper. The verb Shalem, or its noun form of Shalom, convey a sense of something made complete. It is a typical Jewish greeting and farewell. But even this is a shallow understanding of this word.

To the Jewish people, the Lord made all things in the Earth for Adam to enjoy. This state of union with the Father was broken by his disobedience in eating the fruit, but our blessed Redeemer returned us to this state of fellowship. To the Hebrew speaker to speak Shalom over a person is to remind them of this state of all things in Earth being made for him to enjoy, but foremost it's the return of our fellowship with the Father in heaven.

Shalem is also used to describe the unbroken stones of the altar and temple. It was used to denote a righteous wage in the book of Ruth. This word is both an action and state of being. It is not good enough to have peace and wholeness, but one must also make peace or become peaceful to be made whole. To the Hebrew people, peace making started with relationship making, and to understand wholeness one must understand the mind and motives of those who are divided from you.

For our Lord Jesus to have said, "Blessed are the peacemakers" He meant blessed are those who are relationship makers. Those who make relationships between men and Myself. Most interestingly this verb shalem indicates that making peace brings people into relationship, all the while retaining their individuality.

What is there to see then in this little Shulamite? A dance before two factions, the kingdom of darkness desires to steal, kill, and destroy. The devil hates man and desires that all would join him in the pit, but our Lord was victorious over death. This dance of joy before the devil is accomplished when we bring those who are without Christ into the kingdom of light. This is always done by love and through relationship. Shalom.

It is worth noting in the Hebrew text that this verse is not marked as belonging in the sixth chapter, but it is placed as chapter 7 verse 1. The number seven always signified the beginning of rest and completeness since the Lord took His rest on the 7th day of creation. The day of rest and the source of your rest begins with knowing that you are made complete through the cross of Christ. No truer rest can be found than in knowing you have right standing with the Father in heaven.

How does making relationships make peace?

Read Romans 10:14-15

Who has beautiful feet?

Read 2 Samuel 6:14-15

What did David do before the Lord? Why did he rejoice and dance?

Read Exodus 15:20

What does the dance of Miriam signify?

1 Corinthians 15:25

Who is under our feet?

Prayer: Lord, You say 'blessed are the peacemakers'. Help me to focus on the One who is the Prince of Peace and not on my own strength. Make me fit for the purpose You've called me to and help me be a relationship maker with a heart for the lost. In Jesus name, amen.

Activation: In your journal, write down your thoughts on peace maker vs. relationship maker. How might these be similar and how are they different? Have you felt as though you've been helping form and make relationships between people and God? How might your view of witnessing change with this view?

PART 3

Mature Love: Song of Solomon 7:1-8:4

CHAPTER 7

Living a Life of Discipleship

Striving Together

[Then her companions began noticing and commenting on the attractiveness of her
person] How beautiful are your feet in sandals, O queenly maiden! Your rounded limbs are
like jeweled chains, the work of a master hand.

The Song of Songs 7:1

The world came to know the Father through the Son, and the world will know the Son through His followers. It is no surprise then that these attributes are extolled in this maiden. The bridegroom praises her, from the soles of her feet to the top of her head, and notes all the things which make her a true disciple of Christ.

It's no longer just Christ in her that He praises, but her willingness to abandon all her will for the will of the Father. While the bride describes her bridegroom from head to foot, we see she is described in reverse. Just as a mirror reverses the image, we find she is in fact a living image of the Lord and a daughter with an inheritance.

Supernatural ability and provision will always accompany those who follow the will and leading of the Father. The princes' daughter should always be arrayed with the knowledge that there are those without a relationship with her bridegroom, and be ready with the gospel of peace for their weary hearts. It is the path we tread on a daily basis, to be more and more transformed into His image and follow the path He sets before us.

Links of chain form a strong cohesive unit, and here the bride joins together the saving knowledge of the gospel and the strength of knowing truth. The truth is Christ not only saved us, but set us free. The work of the entire body of Christ is to bring increase to the kingdom and the thighs are responsible for the motion of the body. These strong links with other believers allow her to move and work effectually within the larger body.

The joining of our lives to Christ is part of the Father's plan put into place long before the foundations of the world. Our Father sees the end from the beginning. The stories of our lives are the design of a master craftsman. All believers are placed in the body exactly as God intends (1 Corinthians 12:18).

Do you belong to a company of believers? Why do you believe God has placed groups of people together?

Read Isaiah 52:7

Where do those with beautiful feet walk? Who leaps upon the mountains in Songs 2:8?

Read Hebrews 10:25

Why should we regularly assemble with others? When are we especially instructed to do so?

Read Philippians 1:27

How is the body to conduct itself? For what purpose?

Prayer: Lord, Your plan is perfect and magnificent. I praise You for the body of Christ and each believer who is a part. I pray for unity within the body and for all members to grow in wisdom and knowledge of Your will. Let us all join together for the gospel and give You glory for growth in Jesus name, amen.

Activation: Are you a part of a local body of believers? Take time today to pray for each member of your local body, that they would be in unity of purpose and spirit. The enemy knows that believers in unity are effective against Him and tries daily to cause schism and division. If you aren't a part of a local body, ask the Lord where you can plug in and begin walking together with others for the gospel.

Set with Lilies

Your body is like a round goblet in which no mixed wine is wanting. Your abdomen is like a heap of wheat set about with lilies.

The Song of Songs 7:2

This mixed wine was a blend of water and wine. The wine described earlier was always the fermented wine used in banqueting. The wine goblets containing the wine were placed upon the table of show-bread before the Lord and were used as the source of wine for the daily offering.

We are temples of the Holy Spirit through Christ, and our joining with Him in his divine nature joins together these facets of our lives, the wine of sacrifices and the water of life. It is symbolic of our joining with the Holy Spirit. This mixed wine could never be separated again just as we can never be separated from our bridegroom.

It should be no surprise to us that the first of Jesus' many miracles was the turning of water into wine at the wedding in Canna. In John chapter 2, we see Mary approach Jesus with the quandary that all the wine was gone for the wedding feast. Jesus replied that his time had not yet come to be revealed, but He chose to perform this miracle for the guests and all those who would read its account.

Marriage in Jewish tradition was one of the largest celebrations in a person's life. The feast was held in the home of the bridegroom's Father. The containers which he ordered filled with water were for the purpose of purification. Israel at this time was without the wine of sanctification, and all were waiting for the Messiah's arrival to free them from the oppression of Rome.

How opportune that Mary carefully point out that the guests were lacking, and the answers to their deepest desire was in fact sitting in their midst. His address to her of 'woman my time has not come' is neither a slight nor is it condescending. The true ministry of our Lord was not to free us of earthly oppression but to 'crush the head' of the serpent who deceived Eve, setting us free of every spiritual and natural hindrance. That final victory had not yet been won, but it is the pattern of God to show the end from the beginning. Our Lord provided the wine of sacrifice in this first wedding feast foreshadowing the final miracle of the marriage supper with our Lamb.

We have a position in the kingdom in a place of honor and authority. We have answers with the gospel of peace, and provision with the Bread of Life which we carry. The bread and mixed wine nourish us and others daily with truth.

Why is it important to read the praises of the bridegroom toward the bride? What impact does this have on you and your view of discipleship?

Read Psalm 81:16
What is this wheat the Lord would feed the people with? Why does it say honey out of the rock when water gushed from it in Exodus?

Read John 6:48
What does Jesus call himself?

Read Hosea 14:4-6

Who is speaking in these verses? What will He do? What will happen to those He heals?

Prayer: I praise You and thank You Lord for the Word and Holy Spirit. I pray and ask for Your guidance and wisdom how to balance them in my life. Let me know and understand truth and experience renewal and refreshing in Jesus name, amen.

Activation: Living with a balance of Word and Spirit can be difficult. Often, we approach one with ease and have difficulty understanding the other. Ask the Lord today how you can effectively balance knowing the Word and experience the moving of the Spirit. Write down what you hear in your journal, and focus this week on applying these words to your life.

Nourishing New Believers

Your two breasts are like two fawns, the twins of a gazelle.

The Song of Songs 7:3

To nurture and nourish those who are new in Christ is a great call. We should take care with those who have just decided to make Jesus their Lord. Most are hungry for more, but they are unable to process the wonders of His grace and mercy when newly reborn. The company is saying here that she helps nourish those who need Him in the correct way.

How should we help encourage new believers? Paul writes in his letter to the Corinthian church that he teaches them the most basic beliefs of Christianity because they still are carnal and think with minds of the world. Those basic beliefs are repentance, baptism, healing, resurrection, and the judgement seat of Christ.

While the law was fulfilled, and the tablets of Moses are written on our hearts, we are called to be priests and kings of the kingdom, leading others along the path of righteousness.

To lead others, one must understand how to guide those believers in the basics of living life for Christ.

Repentance is the beginning of all change in believers. We are born into this world of sin, and our lives adapt and conform to its wickedness. It's easy to simply share the love of Christ with others, but it's often harder to share the need for true heartfelt repentance. Our flesh is selfish and pointing out the sinfulness of its desires and the need for change can cause many believers pause.

To share the need for true repentance with the world, one must first understand what it is. The first step of repentance is conviction, or understanding what is right and wrong. The Word of God is our source of all truth and good, and conviction is sharing the truth of the Good News. By sharing this truth, the Holy Spirit can begin pointing out how a person has gone the wrong way.

The next step is having Godly sorrow as Paul describes in 2 Corinthians chapter 7. This regret of sin brings about a desire to change or repent of our ways. True repentance will cause one's heart to cry 'Abba Father' and make a decision for the Lord Jesus. Leading people along this path of repentance can be challenging, but it's good to remind ourselves that our most powerful tool in sharing Christ is our testimony.

Baptism of believers in water is more than laying down the old man and rising up a new creation. Jesus was baptized by John in Matthew chapter 3. Though John argued it was Christ who should be baptizing him, Jesus said it was being done to honor the Father. To understand why Jesus needed to be immersed, we must understand the Hebrew tradition behind immersion.

The pattern of betrothal and marriage customs demanded that the Father of the bridegroom choose a wife for his son. The Father would negotiate the terms of marriage and send his son along with a *ketubah*, or contract, to the bride's home. This contract or covenant would stipulate all the promises of the bridegroom for the bride and lay out her responsibilities as a betrothed bride.

Before the bridegroom presented himself, he would immerse fully in water, perform *mikveh*, as a sign of spiritual cleansing. This was necessary, as the bridegroom wished to show his bride that the former life was passing away and new life as two become one would begin. We as the bride of Christ also immerse ourselves after making Jesus our Lord. This life of sin and death has passed away, and we awaken to new life as His precious bride.

Healing was paid for at Calvary (1 Peter 2:24). This healing is multifaceted. Not only did our redemption heal the broken relationship between the Father and men, it also paid for the healing of our souls and bodies. The book of Acts is full of instances of the body laying hands on the sick and seeing them recover.

All the gospels declare the great power of our Lord to heal and set us free, and the church as His hands and feet should do the same. As we pray and see the sick recover, the call to salvation is strong. Healing broken hearts and broken bodies will draw people to the loving God who has supplied all their needs.

Resurrection life in Christ is one of victory and joy. The old man has passed away and believers are new creations in Him. Jesus said in John 11, "I am the resurrection and the life." To be in Christ is to live a life triumphant over death. It's a peace of heart and mind that when this life ceases, we will be with Jesus in glory.

The judgement seat of Christ intimidates and brings fear to many, but we must properly understand it if we are to live our lives fully for Him. Paul wrote the believers in Rome and spoke at length about the necessary judgement of Christ (Romans 14:10). We know this isn't a judgment for sin, so we must ask what is the judgment seat for? According to Romans it's 'to give an account for ourselves'.

Every day we each have an opportunity to deny ourselves and take up our cross. To deny this necessary step of discipleship isn't without consequence. We are told in 1 Corinthians 3 that these judgements are determined by our building upon the rock. Did we expand the kingdom by being His hands and feet? Did we share the truth of God's love when we saw people in need?

The judgement seat should be a time of great rejoicing for all believers, but some may find they enter eternity having only escaped the fires of hell having done little God called them to. This truth emphasizes the need for mature mentors. It's the work of the whole body to train up new creations in the truth of God's Word, for to neglect this task is to impair the function of the whole body.

Are there any areas of belief you find yourself unsure of or lacking in knowledge? Ask the Lord for wisdom and revelation in those areas.

Read 1 Corinthians 3:1
What distinguishes a nonspiritual man? Can believers be nonspiritual? How should we teach them?

Read Matthew 28:19-20
What ministry are believers called into? Have you performed this ministry?

Read the Parable of the Talents Matthew 25:14-28
What words were received by the servant with five and two talents? Did the amount of talents matter in the praise they received? What was said to the servant with one talent? What comment did this servant make about his master? Did this servant know his master?

Prayer: Thank you Jesus for being the firm foundation on which I can stand. I ask for wisdom how to help others build the foundation of truth in their hearts. Let all I do and say be for your glory in Jesus name, amen.

Application: Do you feel like you have a firm foundation? Are there any areas discussed above that have seemed confusing? Take time to think on these areas today. Write down any questions you have about repentance, healing, baptism, or the judgement seat. Ask the Lord for clarity and sound doctrine, and see Him answer all your questions in amazing ways.

Inner Peace

Your neck is like a tower of ivory, your eyes like the pools of Heshbon by the gate of Bath-rabbim. Your nose is like the tower of Lebanon which looks toward Damascus.

The Song of Songs 7:4

Earlier in this song, the neck of the bride is likened to the tower of David, which was fortress secured for battle, and her defenses were mighty. Here we see her neck as a graceful pillar of ivory. It is a change that happens in our lives, when we finally see ourselves not as warriors who must battle the devil, but as victorious conquerors who have already won. Our fight is not against the flesh and blood we see, but it is against the principalities of darkness who seek to deceive us (Ephesians 1:21).

What do we fight then if we are already victorious? Our fight is similar to Jacob's when he wrestled with the angel and said, "I will not let go until you've blessed me" (Genesis 32:26). Our fight is for the grace, the revelation, the knowledge of who we already are in Christ. Our fight is to make this secure in our head and heart that we are above and not beneath, the head not the tail, the overcomer who is loved by her bridegroom.

Those mysteries and secrets that pertain to our lives that are found in Him are not only for knowing our call and the things we are to do in this life. They are revelations and graces to overcome the thoughts and emotions that circle our minds reminding us of our past and our sin. If the devil can convince us of our inadequacy, he will defeat the plan of God in us, for we can only move forward in the plan He has for us when we believe we are worthy and capable of finishing.

Heshbon was a city set aside for the Levites of the tribe of Gad. It was a city in which any person could find rest from accusation; it was called a sanctuary city. Within this sanctuary were pools that provided refreshing for the weary since they were deep and still. Bath-Rabbim translates as Gates of the Daughter of the Many. Our life in Him is a product of many before praying continually and praising without ceasing.

Pools show reflections just as we are to reflect the image of Christ. Here her eyes, or her way to perceive and see, are seeing through His perspective. The pools gaze toward the heavens constantly as her source of knowing. Before, her dove's eyes were able to fix upon certain aspects of her bridegroom, now those eyes are larger and can encompass His entire ascended person. The pools not only reflect but are located near the gate and witness all the coming and going of the city.

This setting near the gate is so vital for the church body. It's imperative that mature believers keep close watch on the comings and goings of those who preach, teach, and lead. This nose toward Damascus is a symbol of spiritual intuition. Like a bloodhound, we must always be seeking the foul smell of wolves who parade as sheep.

Have you ever experienced the feeling of someone or something 'off' in the body? What did the sense tell you?

Read Psalm 59:17

Who is our strong tower? How does this strong tower enable us to rest?

Read Titus 1:1

What did Paul wish to impart through teaching? What does this teaching lead to?

Read Matthew 11:39

What is the promise for those who labor with the Lord?

Prayer: Father in heaven, help me keep my eyes turned toward You. Let all I see before me pale in comparison to the wonders of Your love, grace, and mercy. I pray for discernment and spiritual wisdom for myself and all those within the body in Jesus name, amen.

Application: Discernment and wisdom are necessary for so many issues we face. We find ourselves faced with decisions daily that require a constant stream of communication with the Father. Do you have a problem or situation you're facing that needs an answer from heaven? Take time today to ask the Lord for discernment and wisdom for that situation. Write down all you hear or anything that you read today which helps you make a decision.

A Crown Upon the Head

Your head crowns you like Mount Carmel, and the hair of your head like purple. The king is held captive by its tresses.

The Song of Songs 7:5

To the people of Solomon's day, the head was not merely a part of the body, it was considered the principle part of the body. It's easy to understand when we know the mind controls all things the body does. Here the implication is the principle part crowns us, just as Mount Carmel crowns the valleys below. Christ is the head of the church, and it is He who crowns us as Carmel. All wisdom and knowledge are gained when we view our lives with Him as our source of answers.

Who could possibly hold a king captive? Acar, translated here as held, means not only captive but held bound, fettered in chains, put in prison. It is used throughout the Word to describe one who is completely subject to the whims and authority of another.

Everything from the manner in which we walk, the way we stand, the way we disciple new believers, the way we keep our gaze upon Him; those are the things which the King finds beautiful. The first usage of this word in scripture is in the story of Joseph when he was imprisoned in Egypt.

We know how Joseph's story ends. It's often too easy to overlook those years in prison. How difficult is it to trust God when everything around us seems to fall apart? We have dreams of great works done for the kingdom, and life happens. We know His word is true, yet here we sit seeming to never move forward. Joseph must have asked himself the same questions we all ask ourselves. Is God really in control here? Where did I go wrong? Does God really have a plan for my life?

Joseph is a marvelous parallel of our Lord in scripture. In Genesis 37, we read of his great gift of the coat of many colors. He was his Father's favorite son. He was stripped of this glory when he was sold and sent to Egypt as a slave. However, we see even in this state he worked diligently and was given many favors because of his wisdom and knowledge.

His story turns again when he overcomes the temptation of Potiphar's wife only to be thrown into prison after being falsely accused. After a time, he was brought out exalted and even enthroned as second only to Pharaoh himself. Joseph was then given a new name, all authority, and soon controlled the distribution of bread to all who came. We see in scripture, this bread never ran out. Most important for us today is the fact Joseph was given a gentile bride.

Isn't it true we were all once prisoners in Egypt? The land of Egypt represents the world and the world's system in scripture. We were all once enslaved by it, but our bridegroom bought us with a price and brought us into the kingdom of light. Even Christ left the heavenly habitation and lived as a man so we may be His bride. Jesus is saying to us, "I have willingly bound myself to my gentile bride."

Describe the faithfulness of Joseph. How is he an example of Christ?

Read James 2:18

What works accompany faith? How is Jesus glorified by our works?

Read Jeremiah 29:11

What plans does the Lord have for us? How does this give us confidence before God?

Read 1 John 3:19-22

Why must we be reassured? Who accuses us of being guilty? Why is our conscious clean?

Prayer: Lord, I pray now for strength to stand firm before the attacks of the enemy. I know I am an overcomer and that You have started a work in me You promised to finish. Help me fight the good fight of faith. Even when I can't see, Your promises are always yes and amen. I praise You for the victory in Jesus name, amen.

Application: The strongest weapons we carry are the name of Jesus and the Word. In the wilderness, Satan tempted the Lord and He overcame by speaking the truth of the Word. Do you have verses memorized for when the enemy attacks? Search the Word of God today for verses to memorize and hold on to. When the enemy comes with accusations or lies, speak the truth!

Delights

How fair and how pleasant you are, O love, with your delights!

The Song of Songs 7:6

Though the King is held bound and captive by his bride, He says to her how wonderful it is to belong to her. Do you know how earnestly the Lord desires you?

After Joseph interpreted the dream of Pharaoh and was made second in the land of Egypt, Pharaoh gave to him Asenath. Her name means 'of the goddess Neith', and her Father was the priest of Heliopolis. All her life she was exposed to the pagan life of the priests of Egypt, but God knew her even in the depths of her spiritual darkness.

Asenath would know nothing of the God of Abraham, but she was chosen by a sovereign to be the wife of Joseph. With no work of her own she shared in the abundant life her husband's position provided. The life of Asenath embodies of the glory of the church and the grace bestowed upon us by God.

While we were sinners Christ died for us, but not only did He save us He elevated us with Him. He gave us new life through a new birth and placed our lives in Him. Through Christ, the whole body is raised together and given a distinction among the nations. Asenath was also given a distinction by her husband. She was the only wife of Joseph in a land where polygamy was the norm.

In a time where a man in this position could have many wives, it is a testimony to her husband's faithfulness. Asenath also bore Joseph two sons, whose names replaced those of both Joseph and Levi when the tribes of Israel were named. The God of grace lifted her to a place of prominence without striving and effort, and made her an heir of the kingdom with two tribes tracing their roots to her.

Manasseh was the eldest child of Asenath. Manasseh means forgetting, but not in the sense one just doesn't remember or recall. Rather it is a word used to describe the way a puddle of water evaporates and ceases to exist. The Father tells us in several places in the New

Testament, our sins are forgotten. When God says our sins are forgotten, it isn't as though He can't recall, but He causes those things to cease to exist.

The name Ephriam is interesting to translate. It means fruitful, but fruitfulness in Jewish tradition is not simply multiplication, it inherently means to split or cut and re-root to multiply.

A root verb of this word talks about the multiplication of people and animals which takes part of one's self and joins it to another part. This deep understanding of fruitfulness, equating to sharing one's self with another to produce life, brings a deeper knowledge of all Christ does for us. He is the part that joins our lives and helps to make us fruitful by multiplying His kingdom.

Describe the first instance you can clearly remember the love of God reaching out to you before salvation.

Read Isaiah 62:5
Who does the Lord rejoice over?

Read 2 Corinthians 4:13-14
What does faith allow us to say? Does this promise require works?

Read Ephesians 1:11
We are given an inheritance as believers. Who gives it to us? Who gives us access to this inheritance? Why are we given one?

Read Ephesians 2:5

When were we made alive in Christ? How is this made possible?

Prayer: Lord, I need your grace daily. Help me honor and love those I see, and let my heart be moved by Your desire for them. You are my shepherd, guide me in everything I do and say today in Jesus name, amen.

Application: Thinking back to your first encounter with Christ, what aspect of salvation made the most impact on your decision to make Jesus your Lord? Take time today to speak with the Father about what drew you to Him. Do you still find yourself drawn? Is it for the same reason, or have your reasons for deepening your relationship with Him changed?

Righteous Growth

Your stature is like that of a palm tree, and your bosom like its clusters.

The Song of Songs 7:7

Few trees anywhere can claim the stature of a palm. The upright ever-branching nature is just one of its many important traits. The growth of the palm tree is made upright by its bearing fruit. The weight of the fruit causes the fibers in the trunk to tighten and strengthen it. The constant wind the ocean breezes produce buffets them and helps the palm to grow strong.

Its roots dig deep to find sources of water. These same fibers in the trunk allow the tree to bend in hurricanes without breaking. The fronds drop on a yearly basis, which opens the ground beneath them to the sun, meaning they never inhibit any growth under them. This shedding of fronds also keeps the crown of the tree looking healthy and green. While so many other trees branch out and appear fruitful and pleasant, only the palm reaches upward directly to heaven.

At the heart of the palm tree's life is the fact it grows in areas where there is little moisture. Even growing in the harsh conditions they face, the palm tree is exceedingly fruitful. Many trees produce in upwards of 300 pounds of fruit in one harvest season. Though there are times we feel the world is barren around us and our mission field isn't showing signs of life, we are still fruitful for the kingdom. Just as the Israelites journeyed through the wilderness, there are times and seasons of refreshing and abundance.

To the Hebrews, the palm tree is a symbol of the tree of life in the garden. The date palm has been a symbol of the tribe of Judah for millennia. It was along the journey through the wilderness they came upon the encampment of Elim with its twelve wells and seventy palm trees. Elim means uprightness, much like the palms growing in the oasis. The wells nourished the people and the shade of the palms provided much needed relief.

This journey through the desert should have lasted a few weeks, but it was forty years before they entered the land and first took the city of Jericho, or Ir-hatamarim, the City Of Palms in Deuteronomy 24:3. The wickedness of the generation and the mentality of slavery to Egypt had to die in this place of barrenness before God's people could be allowed into the promised land.

Once they crossed over the Jordan they entered into the promise the Lord swore to Abraham. This city of palms was the first to come into their hands, and with it the knowledge that God was their security and promise. Israel was called the land of milk and honey, but it was not a honey produced by bees. The honey gathered by the early inhabitants of the land was really the sap of the palm tree.

The palm was also vital part of the celebration of Sukkot. It was a reminder of the blessings of harvest in the land they resided, and the providence of God in their wilderness journey. They resided in shelters built from the palm trees and waved the branches in all directions as prayer and thanksgiving.

On the seventh day of Sukkot, they offered prayers for rains, and an offering of water from the Pool of Siloam was poured out on the temple altar. Jesus taught on this day of Sukkot and said in John 7:37, "If anyone thirsts, let him come to me and drink. Whoever believes in me, as the Scripture says, 'Out of his heart will flow rivers of living water.'"

This comparison to the palm tree holds many meanings for the bride of Christ. We walk in shoes of His gospel of peace and help raise up others through discipleship. We must be ready to endure winds and dry places in multiplying His kingdom, for Satan does his best to keep the world in darkness. To succeed in bringing the kingdom, we must also understand the necessity of looking toward heaven at all times and digging deeper into the person of Jesus Christ for the source of refreshing.

Have you endured circumstances that tried to topple you? How did you endure?

Read Exodus 15:25-27
What miracle takes place? What is the promise given to the Israelites? Number the springs of water and palm trees.

Read James 1:2-3How can we consider it joyful to be surrounded by tests and trials? What do these trials produce?
Read Psalm 92:19 Who are the righteous? What is their promise from the Father?

Prayer: Father, I thank You for the cover of Your wings in time of trouble. No matter what I face, You are always there to comfort, cover, and protect. You are a good Father who loves His children, and I praise You every day for loving me. In Jesus name, amen.

Application: David was a man after God's own heart. Every time he faced challenges and odds that overwhelmed him, he would turn to the Lord and sing a song of praise. Take time today to praise the Lord.

Fruits of the Bride

I resolve that I will climb the palm tree; I will grasp its branches. Let your breasts be like clusters of the grapevine, and the scent of your breath like apples,

The Song of Songs 7:8

The word of God gives us an example of the bride of Christ in Deborah the Prophetess. Many translate the name Deborah to mean the insect bee, but her name is far more complex and prophetic for the body of Christ. The root ר , pronounced dabar, means to formalize with speech. To the Hebrews, in order to establish something as real, one must speak a truth out loud. The speaking of this truth causes it to become real in the mind of the person who hears.

It is why God spoke the universe into existence and why man had to be named. Deborah the prophetess was so named because she needed to speak out loud the truth of God's Word as the Israelites went astray. We too are called to speak the truth of Christ's death and resurrection and make it real to those who hear.

Deborah, wife of Lapidoth, judged from under the palm tree in Ephraim between Ramah and Beth-el. Ramah, which means the apex of something in height, like the high places of idol worship, and Beth-el, meaning the house of God. She judged Israel after the prophet Ehud had died.

The union between Israel and the Father was broken by the nation again returning to evil ways of idolatry. However, He was still speaking to the faithful prophetess in the land under the palm, who chose her place away from the idol places and on the path toward His habitation.

By our very nature, we are made to worship the Father in heaven, and oftentimes we replace God with other things. To the Father, idolatry is something we place first in our lives instead of Him. What do we love first? Do we love our things? Our time? Our children? Our spouse? What does it mean for us in our walk with the bridegroom?

Often, we find ourselves wondering why things don't happen as planned, or why we never experience a breakthrough in our lives. Deborah was placed under the palm tree to judge Israel and teach the truth of repentance and turning away from idols. She brought to remembrance that the nation had been given by God to the seed of Abraham, and as such, it was necessary to take it back from the evil king who oppressed them.

She did this not to upset a natural order, but to emphasize a spiritual truth we must know. We seek first the kingdom and we will be set free from anxiety, stress, and toil. At this time, it was the deepest wish of the people to be set free of oppression, but to be set free we must first let go of what we hold on to so tightly. Do we let go of those things, or do we hold on out of fear, envy, or anger?

Each time we allow more of the old man in us to pass away, the more Jesus is found in us. Many are afraid of handing over their children, time, and things to God, but He is good and gives us all good things. Where is God? What is He doing? How do I respond?

The palm branches in scripture are carried by the multitude in Revelation 7 as a symbol of justice and by the worshipers at Sukkot as a sign for the provision in the wilderness. This feast of Tabernacles is also symbolic of the second coming of Christ. The justice of god will silences the accuser, and the joy of the Lord through thankfulness will be our strength to overcome. When we overcome we are doubly fruitful and our whole countenance shows it.

The double fruits, or the fruit multiplied here, are the grapes and apples. Earlier we saw the bride describe her bridegroom as the apple tree in the woods. This type of Christ was not arrayed like the other trees, but it was one created and nourishing to others like it by seed.

To become one who sows the Word and brings others into relationship with Him, we must partake of what we intend to share. Do we feast on the fruit of His Word and resurrection? The truth is, many wait for God to intervene on their behalf, but it is our responsibility to search the Word for its truth.

Do you feel the Lord has first place in your life? What other people or things have held that place?

Read Corinthians 2:2

What was Paul's purpose in teaching the believers in Corinth?

Read Luke 12:31

How does one seek first the kingdom? What will be provided?

Read Judges 4:5

A righteous judge rendered decisions based on the wisdom of God. Why did the Israelites go to Deborah?

Read Psalm 107:9

How would the Lord perform this verse through believers?

Read Revelation 7:9

The palm branches of Sukkot were waved as a sign of victory and assurance. What did the multitude overcome?

Read Matthew 26:27-29

What is the wine symbolic of? When will Jesus partake again? How does this relate to multiplied fruit of the bride?

Prayer: You, Eternal One, are a deep sea, into which the more I enter, the more I find, and the more I find, the more I seek. My soul cannot be satisfied in Your abyss, for it continually hungers after You. Oh Lord, what more could You give me than Yourself? Clothe me with eternal truth, so that I may run this life in true obedience with the light of Your most holy Word. – Catherine of Siena

Application: Our life in Him is secure yet ever changing. Paul describes this as growing from glory to glory. Take time today to think back on all you have learned and grown in through this study and other studies you've done. Write down your thoughts in your journal. Praise Him for the promise that as we seek Him, we find Him.

The Best Kisses

"And your kisses like the best wine" "That goes down smoothly and sweetly for my beloved gliding over his lips while he sleeps!"

The Song of Songs 7:9

We continue to progress toward our ultimate goal of the kisses from His mouth, and knowing His breath, speech, and command in our lives. Time can't quench our desire to know His every word to us, and for us. Here the Bridegroom tells us our mouth is the best sacrifice and offering.

The bride interrupts the bridegrooms' speech with her own declaration that this wine goes down sweetly. The word she uses to describe this path the wine takes, מֵישָׁר *meyshar*, is an interesting choice. It can describe the straight or upright path something or someone may take.

214

Often it describes a way considered just and upright before the Lord. Its first usage is found in first chronicles when David dedicated the temple to God and rejoiced with Israel that the house of the Lord was finished and ready for worship.

The upright who worship the Lord in spirit and truth do far more than sing songs of praise. While worship may include songs or hymns, it is the prostration of our lives before Him that is true worship. In Genesis, worship is first mentioned by Abraham when he tells the servants he and Isaac were to worship the Lord and return (Gen22:5).

They climb the mountain, build an altar, and Abraham prepares to sacrifice his son. This connection of worship with sacrifice is significant as it is the first mention found in the Bible. The first usage of a word in scripture becomes our blueprint for how we should view the future uses of the Word as we read and meditate.

One may believe sacrifices were done away with when Jesus died on the cross, however; we see this isn't entirely true. While it is true the blood sacrifices of the old testament are no longer offered, for Jesus was our perfect atoning sacrifice, we find within the letters of Paul it was only the nature of the thing sacrificed that differed once Christ had offered himself.

In Romans, the apostle Paul speaks at length of the sacrifices we make daily as believers.

Romans 12:1: "I exhort you, therefore, brothers, in view of God's mercies, to offer yourselves as a sacrifice, living and set apart for God. This will please him; it is the logical "Temple worship" for you." (The Complete Jewish Bible)

Our very lives, daily lived in obedience to the will of the Father, is our worship. It is the prostrating of our lives before Him who knows the end from the beginning. To worship in Spirit is to live this life daily attuned to the leading of the Holy Spirit. Do we share a compliment to that woman over there? Do we notice the limp of the man there and stop to pray for healing? Do we offer a word of encouragement to our bank teller?

Living a life in worship and reverence to the Holy Spirit inside us will change lives and further the kingdom of God. He sees the hearts of men, and with our living temple being sacrificed to His will, they will see the goodness of God and rejoice.

This truth causes the lips of those asleep in the rest of the Lord to move. This sleep is the perfect rest of Jesus. The joy in our hearts for the sacrifice He made causes our lips to continually give Him praise.

Why is worship a sacrifice? What have you sacrificed in worship to the Lord?

Read 1 Chronicles 29:17
What does the Lord delight in? What brought David joy in this verse?

Read Proverbs 8:6-8
Describe the words of a righteous man.

Read Psalm 150
Where should we praise the Lord? Why do we praise Him? What do we praise Him with? Who is called to praise the Lord?

Read Romans 15:5-7
What is Paul's prayer for the church? Why does he so desire they live in harmony and unity?

Prayer: Father, I pray today for wisdom and revelation how I should live in harmony and unity with my brothers and sisters in Christ. Knit our hearts together so we strive together for Your glory and for the gospel of Jesus Christ. Show us the just and upright way we are to walk and talk in Jesus name, amen.

Application: Unity and harmony with others can be difficult, especially when we have differing opinions of ideas of how to do kingdom work. Have you found it difficult to work alongside some fellow believers? Ask the Lord today for ideas how you can work in harmony with others. Be sure to pray for open hearts and clear words so there are no misunderstandings.

Perfect Love

[She proudly said] I am my beloved's, and his desire is toward me!

The Song of Songs 7:10

Perfect love takes hold in this bride's heart. No longer does she claim any type of ownership of her Bridegroom, but she knows and understands His perfect love is one of desire. Desire is a stretching toward or longing for something, and this particular word is only used three times in scripture. This word in Hebrew תְּשׁוּקָ (tĕshuwqah) comes from the root שׁוּק shûwq, meaning to overflow like water.

Throughout the gospels, Jesus calls Himself the living water. Out of the abundance of life, the water flows to all believers. His desire is that we find our source and only supply in Him, and He desires our heart always seek His nourishment first. This isn't out of duty or law, but out of love and free will.

Christ is not an object the church may possess, but rather he is the head of the church who graciously guides and leads us in our union. For a better understanding, we must look at the word *toward*. The bride is stating she is her beloved's wholly without reservation, but she notes His longing and desire is toward her.

217

Toward in this statement is a preposition. It relates two objects together and how they are related, in this instance, desire and me. The desire for her implies He has something to give her. This longing to have something for her is noted by the Apostle Paul in Ephesians

Ephesians 1:18-19: " *I pray that* the eyes of your heart may be enlightened, so that you will know what is the hope of His calling, what are the riches of the glory of His inheritance in the saints, 19 and what is the surpassing greatness of His power toward us who believe."

The resurrection power toward us who believe is His desire for our resurrection from sin and death. Jesus ascended to the right hand of the Father, and it's His will we know and understand the power of His resurrection in us. Do we understand all things are under our feet? Do we know we have an advocate who silences the enemy? Do we know we are called kings and priests, ministers of the good news?

In the words of Watchman Nee, "We know that our existence is for the purpose of satisfying His desire. Our purpose for living is to be the object of His desire. We are to be the desired ones of the desiring One. The question now is not what we feel, what we gain, what we lose, or what our work is. What is of importance to us is that we are His, and His desire is toward us. This is all that matters."

Have you found it difficult to be the object of the Lord's desire? Why?

Read 1 John 4:9-10

How was the love of God made real? Why was this done?

Read Psalm 51:6

What does the Lord desire? What does David equate this to?

Read Psalm 132:12-13

What does the Lord desire? Why did He choose it?

Read Matthew 9:13

What does the Lord desire?

Prayer: Lord, let my life satisfy you. All I am is Yours, and all I have is Yours. I pray for my heart to be enlightened and to know the desire You have toward me. In Jesus name, amen.

Application: Do you find it difficult to be the object of the Lord's desire? Spend time today with Him and ask for a revelation of the Lord's desire toward you. Write down what you hear in your journal.

The Harvest Fields

[She said] Come, my beloved! Let us go forth into the field, let us lodge in the villages.

The Song of Songs 7:11

God's ways are higher than our ways and He is incomprehensible to our human understanding; however, we can begin to realize the depths of it through His love and His son. When we begin to understand it is His desire to always be with us, it is easy to set aside our ways and follow Him. Here the bride initiated an important journey, echoing what Jesus asks of believers in the Gospel of John when He speaks of bringing in the harvest.

Many mistakenly believe it's the work of ministers and those within the church to share the good news of the gospel, but this is not true. Few ideas have hurt the body of Christ more than the concept of laity. While not all are called to be evangelists, we are all called to be ministers of the gospel (2 Corinthians 3:6).

We are unable to do this work alone, and this is why we see her ask her bridegroom to join her. Each individual believer will have a field to go forth and tend, and each person will do the work differently. While one may pray for a co-worker's sick spouse, another may take a casserole to ease their chore at home. All within the body have a function and purpose. When working together, they bring a person to knowledge of just how much the Father loves them. Then the one who reaps may come and guide them to the Lord for salvation.

To lodge, or לוּן luwn, means to abide or remain in a place. This abiding is done in the villages, but the word used here is particular. It is used in only one other place in scripture in 1 Chronicles 27:25, where it states that apart from the king's treasure the treasuries everywhere else were kept secure by Johnathan, son of Uzziah.

The treasures outside the habitation of the king were no less important to him, and to see this word used again means much more. God has made man in His own image. While fallen man is separated from Him, the desire of His heart is that all would return. These 'treasures' are still outside the kingdom. Only through the body of believers will more enter into His storehouse.

This word village is derived from a word meaning covered or protected. In some sense, it means to cover by forgiving, atoning, or pardoning. It is the bride's desire to go and share the good news of Jesus in the field and to see herself and these new believers abiding in the covering of His atonement.

To see someone making Jesus their Lord and being cleansed of sin causes joy to rise up in every believer's heart. One cannot help but be reminded of their own commitment to the Lord and all He has done for us. This field was once a place of toil and cursed, but it is now beautiful and full of life for the kingdom.

To abide in the villages, one must leave the comforts of home. This can refer to missions work. Have you left comfort to abide with people? What did you learn about yourself?

Read John 4:35-38

What 'fed' Jesus as He walked on this earth? What does the reaper gather? When does he gather? Within the body there are many ways to help in the gathering. How have you helped gather the harvest?

Read Luke 15:10

What do the angels rejoice over?

Read Ephesians 4:16

How does a body function when made up of many individuals? Who is the head of the body?

Prayer: Jesus, You said to preach the gospel throughout all the earth, and I pray that You would empower me to carry this Good News everywhere I go. Let me be effective in sharing, loving toward all, and a vessel empty of any deceit or ulterior motive. Let my lips always be praising Your goodness and redemption in Jesus name, amen.

Application: Thinking of redemption and the joy of another's salvation causes praise to rise up in our hearts. Spend time praising and thanking God for all the ways you have been used to share His love. In your journal, remember to write down the names of people you have witnessed to or prayed for. It's a wonderful reminder to pray for their continued growth in God and for their hearts to turn toward Him.

Keeper of Vineyards

Let us go out early to the vineyards and see whether the vines have budded, whether the grape blossoms have opened, and whether the pomegranates are in bloom. There I will give you my love.

The Song of Songs 7:12

Early in chapter one, the bride noted her mother's sons had made her keeper of the vineyard, but her own she had not kept. It is possible to worry ourselves more with the work others are doing than to concern ourselves with what God calls us to tend. This nature is not borne out of obligation, but a change in her heart. As we mature in Christ, we begin to see the world and people with His heart. Her desire to see the growth in new believers is an outworking of the desire of her bridegroom.

Jesus tells us in John 15, He is the true vine and we are its branches. To hear the words of our Lord comparing us to the branches or stems of this vine, one should take note to how the grapevine grows, to understand its habit is to gain greater wisdom of what He desires in and for each of us.

The main stem of a grapevine is the woody portion or 'trunk' of the vine. It feeds and nourishes all the branches growing from it. Along the trunk are found stems of growth that originate from new buds. Each bud contains three parts, the first of which is the primary growth. The other two parts of the bud serve as a backup to growth damaged by weather or other means.

The primary growth during the first year is in the form of new shoots which form the leaves and tendrils. After a full season's time, flowers form then fruit matures. Each year, new buds form between the stem and leaf growth from the previous year. The implication is clear. We are all given the chance to burst forth in growth while relying on the source of nourishment, but after a time, all believers are to bear fruit for the kingdom and produce new growth.

The Lord gives all a chance to grow and fail. His love guarantees we are not measured by our lack of successes, but by the desire in our hearts to grow again after failure. Many believers feel condemnation for failure in their walk with Christ. It's important to always understand that the only Perfect One came because we could never be perfect. His love for us is never based on performance.

The comparison between the vine and pomegranate emphasizes the difference in believers but also the growth they experience. The word used for pomegranate is old, and its origins are doubtful in many respects, but the word is closely associated with height or a thing that is 'on high'. In the land of Israel, the pomegranate ripens near the new year, Yom Teruah or Rosh Hashanah, and they are considered 'first fruits' of the new year. The literal meaning of Yom Teruah is 'head of the year' and is begun with the sounding of the shofar, causing many to call it the Feast of Trumpets.

Christ is the first fruits of a new creation, and in Him is the whole body of Christ. Searching for these budding new creations in the vine and pomegranate, the bride is searching out ways to help grow others in the nurture and admonition of the Lord (Ephesians 6:4). Maturity in Him will expand our horizon, where we will view the whole earth as our field.

Knowing times and seasons in God's plan is paramount to following His direction and leading. Many times, we find ourselves stuck in a place and we can't make sense of it. The opposition to leaving, or going another way, never abates, but we've felt the Lord leading us. The Lord will give us direction for our future, but the correct time to do those things will only come when we wait upon Him and allow Him to lead us and guide us. It is why when we do the work of the Kingdom the Holy Spirit must go with us.

When you were first born again, how did you view the church? How did you view the lost? Has your view of 'church' and 'the world' changed since then? How?

Read 1 Corinthians 15:20-23

What does it mean that Christ is the first fruits?

Read 1 Thessalonians 5:1-2

Why do you believe it's important to know the times and seasons of Christ's return?

Read Luke 21:34-36

What weighs down and burdens our hearts? Why is it important to not be burdened? What will the unburdened escape?

Read Daniel 12:9-10

Who is purified and white? How does the Lord describe the pure?

Prayer: Open your journal to the names you've written down. Spend time before the Father praying for each of them as the Spirit leads you. Make notes of what you've prayed, and the date. When you see these people again, it's a wonderful way to confirm that your prayers are heard in heaven and answered!

Give God the Glory

The mandrakes give forth fragrance, and over our doors are all manner of choice fruits, new and old, which I have laid up for you, O my beloved!

The Song of Songs 7:13

The word translated mandrakes in this passage is a most peculiar one. The Hebrew word, דּוּדַי *duwday*, has no known roots; its original meaning is lost. It is translated mandrakes in this verse and in Genesis 30.

There was no love lost between sisters Leah and Rachel, one bitter from her husband's neglect, the other barren while her sister bore four sons. Neither are found to be holy in thought or motive in the passage, but some profound truth can be gleaned from their battle.

In the passage, we find Rachel, the barren sister, asking for the plant. In ancient times, it was often used as part of magical practices to cure infertility. Leah scoffs at her sister and asks why she should share the plant when Rachel already enjoys the love of her husband. At this point, Rachel offers to trade a night with Jacob for the use of the plant.

Rachel was placing her faith in the plant to cure her of infertility and didn't see the children Leah bore were a blessing of God's love. They both bartered for intimacy and praise, which can never be bought, instead of offering prayers and supplications to the Father for their pain.

Was her desire for the love of God, or was it for the notoriety of sons for her husband? Why do we desire fruitfulness in our lives? Is it to we expand the Kingdom and bring new believers to Christ? Or do we desire to be seen out in the fields earning praises of men?

The fruitfulness didn't come with the plant as Rachel had hoped. In fact, God blessed Leah again with another son when she gave the mandrakes away. When we see God as the source of our fruitfulness, we don't desire the praises of men, only the praises of our king. It is why we have fruits new and old laid up for Him as they are for His glory.

How do you handle praise from people? Do you find it edifying? How might you balance praise from people vs. praise from God?

Read John 12:43

How does God glorify believers?

Read Philippians 1:11

What is Paul's desire for the church? What are the fruits of right standing? Who should receive honor from this fruit?

Read 1 Thessalonians 2:19-20

Who gave Paul joy and glory? In what did he triumph?

Prayer: Lord, I set before You my heart. I know all praise and glory belong to You. Remind me when the praise of men becomes too much so that all the fruits of my labor are by Your grace alone. I pray that all who I share the name of Jesus with would see Him in me and know that You are good. In Jesus name, amen.

Application: Thanksgiving to God is a common theme in the book of Psalms. As David encountered trials he often praised and thanked God for the victory before the battle took place. It's easy for believers to have this heart of thankfulness when we contemplate all Christ has done for us. Today in your journal, spend time writing all the ways you are thankful for

Jesus. What did He deliver you from? How has your life changed since? Let Him know how thankful you are today.

CHAPTER 8

Abide In Him

Kinsman Redeemer

Oh, that you were like my brother, who nursed from the breasts of my mother! If I should find you without, I would kiss you, yes, and none would despise me [for it].

The Song of Songs 8:1

These words may seem highly unusual for a bride to exclaim to her bridegroom, but as we dig deeper into the meaning of her earnest desire, we find a beautiful epithet of love and affection. Not only does the bride desire a closer and more intimate relationship with the bridegroom, she desires that all could see the kisses He graces her lips with. The need the bride expresses for a close relation also brings to mind the law of kinsman redeemer.

The Word of God gives many examples of the love and faithfulness of our Lord. In the book of Ruth, we see Boaz as a type of Christ acting as a kinsman redeemer. So many read the book of Ruth with its few chapters and never see the amazing truth of what Boaz accomplishes in these four short chapters.

The law of kinsman redeemer allowed a close relative to redeem, or purchase back, the possessions of another lost to debt or sale. It also redeemed individuals who had sold themselves to pay off debts. It coincides in the book of Ruth with the Levirate law, which ensures a possession and an inheritance for the family who lost a son before he could have children.

One might question the nature of the relationship between Boaz and Ruth, as she was a gentile from Moab and became his wife under the fulfillment of the Levirate law, but the truth of his extra covering shown throughout the book gives a clear picture of a much deeper affection of Christ for His gentile bride.

Early in the book, we see Ruth choosing to follow Naomi and making a declaration that is significant for believers today. She makes the decision to follow Naomi and identify herself with the people of Israel and serve their God. She lays aside any past and family in Moab to follow the plan of God for her, and she makes this a decision for the remainder of her life.

This choice mirrors our own decision for Christ. We choose to follow Jesus wherever he leads. We no longer identify with the kingdom of darkness but are now in the Kingdom of light. We worship the Father and fellowship with believers, and our bridegroom Jesus is forever in our hearts. The choice to follow Naomi seemed obvious to Ruth, but it made a clear impact on the inhabitants of Bethlehem when they arrived. The Word states the city was moved about them, literally meaning 'caused an uproar'.

In the second chapter, Boaz meets Ruth for the first time after he left Bethlehem to check on his field during the harvest. After finding her in the field, he instructs her to abide in his field near the maidens who were helping in the harvest. Under the law, anyone who was poor could pick up the dropped grains of wheat or barley or pick at the corners of the field.

Instead of providing Ruth what the law required, Boaz told her to take from the middle of the field alongside the workers; he instructed them to treat her kindly. He told her the water his workers gathered was also available to her. The graciousness of Boaz in providing for a gentile widow didn't stop with gleaning in the field.

Ruth 2:12 May *Adonai* reward you for what you've done; may you be rewarded in full by *Adonai* the God of Isra'el, under whose wings you have come for refuge. (CJB)

When the reapers sat for a meal, Boaz invited her to join them and partake of bread and vinegar. It says she filled herself, but also had enough left over to bring back to Naomi along with an ephah, or bushel, of barley. When Naomi questions where she found so much grain, Ruth explains the grace of Boaz.

The joy of Naomi after hearing this should emphasize just how important it was that Ruth was guided by God to his field. The Kinsman redeemer law was multifaceted and complex since it was not only God's provision for family and welfare, but it was His physical example of all things Jesus would do as our Redeemer.

Revelation 5:1 "And I saw lying on the open hand of Him Who was seated on the throne a scroll (book) written within and on the back, closed *and* sealed with seven seals;"

The scroll of revelation is key to one facet of our redemption through Christ. Notice the scroll is written within and on the back. In old testament times, a sale of property always carried the promise of return to the original owner. Often this was done during the year of Jubilee when all debts were canceled and slaves were set free, but if one accumulated debt and sold property, it was always written on the back of the scroll, the process of redeeming the land through a kinsman.

This scroll in heaven is the deed God gave Adam when he set him in the garden and gave him dominion over all the earth. Adam, through disobedience, lost his dominion to Satan when he disobeyed God. Jesus came as our Kinsman Redeemer to fulfill the obligations on the back of the scroll.

She exclaimed she would embrace him and kiss him, and that those kisses no one would blame her for them, for He is good and deserves all praises for redemption. His kinship with her not only provides her with this sweet redemption from debt to sin, it holds the promise of eternity with the Father.

When did you make the choice to follow Jesus? What were you redeemed from?

Read Hebrews 2:11

Who does Jesus share kinship with? What does it mean to have a 'common origin'?

Read Psalm 111:9

What did God send? How did this take place?

Read Psalm 133

Describe the unity believers have with each other and with Christ.

Prayer: Jesus, I know You are always more than enough. You not only laid down Your life for mine, but You sent the Holy Spirit to comfort me when You ascended to heaven. Thank You, Lord, You more than enough in all areas of my life. Help me hold tightly without wavering to this promise in Jesus name, amen.

Application: Are there areas of your life that seem to lack the 'more than enough' of the Lord? How do you believe this happens? Spend time asking the Father today how to address this issue. Write down all you hear in your journal.

A Personal Savior

I would lead you and bring you into the house of my mother, who would instruct me. I would cause you to drink spiced wine and of the juice of my pomegranates.

The Song of Songs 8:2

As we progress further in the book of Ruth, Naomi instructs Ruth in the law necessary for them to find provision in the land. It is essential to know that in Hebrew culture it was the responsibility of the widow woman to ask for redemption. If a widow did not request it, a kinsman had no obligation to redeem her. Our submission to the Lordship of Christ is done in our hearts. Though it's the will of the Father that none should perish, it's the choice of each person to partake of this redemption.

Ruth not knowing the law needed to be instructed by her mother-in-law on how she should make the request of redemption. Naomi tells her she must prepare and wash herself, then anoint herself and put aside her widow's clothes. A widow's clothing was a sign of her mourning, and for this redemption, her mourning needed to be complete. The joy we all experience at making this choice casts off our filthy garments and clothes us with the righteousness of God in Christ (Revelation 7:14).

Ruth waits until Boaz and his companions are asleep. She then removes his sandals and places the hem of his garment over her own feet. This was necessary as she was making a claim based on the law, she believed him to be her kinsman redeemer. The garment she spread over her feet was a tallit, and at its edges were the knotted tassels signifying all the Law of Moses.

It was not necessary for Ruth to make such a personal claim. A widow only needed to make her claim of redemption known at the city gate in front of the elders, but Boaz was more than an example of law, he is an example of Christ. Our Redeemer is personal, and His claim on us is more than just fulfillment of law. He washes us with the Word and anoints us with the Holy Spirit to lead and guide us in all things.

We acknowledge His Lordship in our lives by repenting of our sin and submitting our will to His, and He covers us with his wings. Just as Boaz handled the matter of Ruth's redemption on her behalf, we do not earn our redemption through Christ by any means other than faith.

Jesus came not only that we would act right, but we would become the righteousness of God. This is an internal action in our hearts and causes our old man to pass away. To know He redeemed us is to appreciate that the law could not save us. A common misunderstanding within the church is that Atonement and Redemption are the same, but this is not true.

Atonement was the covering of sin through sacrifices on an altar, and it could never rid the mind of sin consciousness or guilt. Redemption not only pays the debt once and for all in full, but it rids the debtor of guilt and condemnation. Our redemption paid for all sin past, present, and future. Though we all fall short of the glory of God, our kinsman redeemer has made a way for us to all rise again in pursuit of Him.

How did the Lord reach you before salvation? How did this personal touch of the Savior impact your choice for Him?

Read 1 Peter 1:18-19

What is a ransom? What does this word imply? What purchased us from our captor?

Read Romans 8:16-17

What does the Spirit bear witness of? What are we in Christ?

Prayer: I praise You Jesus! My heart and all I am are Yours. I thank You that You are a personal savior who knows my heart, its weakness, my failures, and my inability, yet at Calvary, You still set me free. Let my life glorify Your sacrifice and Your name in Jesus name, amen.

Application: We have been redeemed! This great salvation and covenant is deemed better because our guilt and shame for our past is gone, but the accuser comes and tries to remind us of our past failures often. Shame and guilt can creep into our lives and put a wedge between us and our bridegroom. Take time today to write out your thoughts and feelings about your relationship with Christ. Do you see any guilt or condemnation? Bring that to the Lord today and ask for His Holy Spirit to work in your heart.

Pillars of the Body

Oh, that his left hand were under my head and that his right hand embraced me!

The Song of Songs 8:3

It is worth noting the left pillar at the entrance of Solomon's temple was named Boaz, or translated from Hebrew 'in him is strength'. The other pillar was Jachin meaning 'established'. We read in 1 Kings 7 that Jachin, the right pillar, was set up first as the head pillar of the temple. The left pillar, Boaz, was raised after. It was the custom in Hebrew tradition, to bless the first born come from the right hand of the Father or grandfather. Here, Jachin symbolizes Christ being the first fruits and the One through whom the church was established.

The pillars of Christ's temple are His redemptive works on the cross. He paid the penalty for our sin and took death, its consequence, and put it under His feet so we might again be free to live as Adam did before the fall. We are free to enjoy communion with the Father in heaven. No longer do we have a separation or veil between us. Each of these pillars were topped with a lily. The bridegroom feeds among the lilies as this temple is where His people are found.

Jesus established the temple, and in Him is strength. How do you find strength in Christ?

Read John 2:19-21
How did Jesus establish the temple?

Read 1 Corinthians 3:16
What do all believers carry?

Read Deuteronomy 33:27-28

How are we temples that find refuge in Him? What does the Lord do to secure us in Him?

Prayer: Lord, I pray that the body of Christ would have wisdom and revelation of who they are in You. Let us join together in unity of mind and purpose for the preaching of the gospel. Let us be pillars of righteousness that proclaim Your glory and victory in Jesus name, amen.

Application: There is no separation between believers and the Father in heaven. Paul tells us in Hebrews to boldly approach the throne of grace to find grace. Boldly approaching isn't believing we deserve to be heard, but is a heart knowledge that we did nothing to earn righteousness in Christ. Approach your prayer this way today. Go to the Father knowing that you are in right standing before Him. Write down your prayers for today and see how God moves when we stand in our rightful place.

Love and Trust

I adjure you, O daughters of Jerusalem, that you never [again attempt to] stir up or awaken love until it pleases.

The Song of Songs 8:4

This verse is nearly identical to songs 2:7 and songs 3:5, though it does not mention gazelles or the does in the field. Instead it's a third command from our bridegroom to never awaken love before its time. The process of loving and trusting the Lord in our lives is similar to our spiritual growth Paul refers to as glory to glory in 2 Corinthians 3:18. The process begins when we repent and make Jesus our Lord.

Though we are not perfect, God beholds us as perfect, because of what Jesus has done in us. We are filled with seeds of 'Christ-likeness', and our new hearts can fulfill Godly desires.

Slowly, the Holy Spirit helps to transform us and lead us in all things. Over time, when we let go of our own will to follow the Father's our actions bring a new testimony all can witness.

Spirit, soul, and body, are the ways we love the Lord. Our spirit is renewed with our decision for Christ, and the Holy spirit begins to work in our lives. Our thoughts change and our lives begin to show the glory of the Lord. Three separate parts all in need of renewal through our bridegroom.

How has the Lord healed your heart, mind, and spirit?

Read Matthew 22:36-38

How do we apply this three-part healing to the great commandment?

Read John 15:10

Where do those who obey this commandment abide?

Read Romans 7:11-13

What does sin do? If the law was good how did sin reign?

Prayer: I praise you Jesus for total renewal in my spirit, soul, and body. I thank You that all things are made new. Holy Spirit, help me to discern and reveal Christ to me in a deeper way in Jesus name, amen.

Application: Early on in chapter 1, you made the goal to read the Bible each day. What have you learned from your experience in reading each day? Did you stick with the plan you made? If the plan you chose didn't work, ask the Lord why and what you should do to make this daily reading a habit.

Part 4: Abiding Love Song of Songs 8:5-8:14

Leaning Wholly

Who is this who comes up from the wilderness leaning upon her beloved? Under the apple tree I awakened you; there your mother gave you birth, there she was in travail and bore you.

The Song of Songs 8:5

Our bridegroom already came up from the wilderness in smoke and perfumes of myrrh, and now the beloved has joined Him and rests fully upon Him for strength. The wilderness journey grows us in ways where we recognize the need for Christ's strength and support in all we do. It is vital we learn to lean and trust in Him completely.

There will be times in our life when we don't understand the opposition or the persecution for His name, but the transformed soul doesn't believe this is a negative experience, just one of growth. The wilderness experience is one every believer must have, and it often arrives in a faith crisis. What do we do when faced with things contrary to the word of God that attack our lives?

Many choose to isolate themselves or begin to blame the crisis on God. James 1 shows us this is the first mistake many believers make. James tells us the tests and trials of faith are evil and God is not behind them. Who then tempts and causes trials of our faith? It is Satan.

While many would admit their belief in God, it is harder to admit Satan is real and our foe. The truth is, those in the world who are still in the kingdom of darkness pose no threat to Satan and his plan, and they are often left complacent by their lacking need for divine intervention.

If they don't feel they lack, why would they cry out to God for salvation? Believers who follow Jesus and wish to share Him with others are a real threat. Though Satan is defeated, it's his wish to deceive many so their names are never written in the Book of Life.

It is not a joyful experience to encounter trials and temptations in the wilderness, but know even Christ was sent to the wilderness to be tempted by Satan. Feelings of abandonment, depression, and heartache are common, often because many feel they have been sent to the wilderness by God for sin, however; we can be assured this is not true.

James 1: 13-14 " Let no one say when he is tempted, I am tempted from God; for God is incapable of being tempted by [what is] evil and He Himself tempts no one.14 But every person is tempted when he is drawn away, enticed *and* baited by his own evil desire (lust, passions)."

To understand the wilderness, let us look closer at words used here. The words 'tempted and try' in the Greek are complex verbs when fully translated mean 'putting a belief, or behavior, to proof by the experience of an adverse circumstance that questions it.' If we understand it is Satan testing us, we realize the wilderness is Satan's attempts at causing circumstances that put to proof our faith in God's word. While Satan does not know our thoughts, many believers fail the test of faith in their words.

James 1:26, "If anyone thinks himself to be religious (piously observant of the external duties of his faith) and does not bridle his tongue but deludes his own heart, this person's religious service is worthless (futile, barren)."

Whatever we are fullest of will spew out our mouths when we are put under pressure by the enemy. It's why the bridegroom points out the apple tree. We must fill our spirit and mind with the word of God daily. As we feast on the Word it changes our hearts and minds so that when we encounter these trials we answer as Jesus did, "It is written".

Our mentors and spiritual elders know when trials come, believers fall away. It happens time and again in the body of Christ. People call upon the Lord joyful that their eternity will be with Him, and later Satan comes with circumstances or unknowing people to put pressure on their faith. Angry at this discomfort, they walk away, never having endured for the lover of their soul. It's why the bridegroom notes the mother has travailed.

All mentors are called to pray for those they help raise up. These prayers are rarely simple blessings. They are often heart-wrenching, tearful pleads before the king for the provision of the Holy Spirit and heavenly wisdom. To lean wholly on Christ is to lean wholly on prayer.

Have you experienced pressure about a particular truth of the Word? How did the test of faith play out?

Read Psalm 9:10

What do those who know the name of the Lord do? Why?

Read Psalm 13:5

What do we lean on? What is our hearts response?

Read Galatians 3:4-6

Do we suffer in vain? Does Christ help us overcome based on our works or our faith? How did Abraham overcome?

Prayer: Lord, no matter what I face, I praise You for the shelter of Your wings. Let my heart not be troubled by the tests and trials of faith the enemy brings. Remind me of the promise that all things work for Your good. Thank You ,Jesus, that You promised to never leave me nor forsake me. In Jesus' name, Amen.

Application: In this place of abiding love, our hearts cry out to praise Him for all He has done. Spend time praising the Lord and thanking Him today.

A Seal Upon My Heart

Set me like a seal upon your heart, like a seal upon your arm; for love is as strong as death, jealousy is as hard and cruel as Sheol (the place of the dead). Its flashes are flashes of fire, a most vehement flame [the very flame of the Lord]!

The Song of Songs 8:6

The bridegroom tells the bride to place a seal over her heart and arm. This request is not out of obligation, but love. Jesus came into the world as the Word of God and used the Word as a weapon in the wilderness and in response to the attacks of the Pharisees. However, He reveals himself to believers in a different way as one desiring relationship.

Many believers never move past the point of seeing Christ as more than insurance from hell, but this 'church going' rather than relationship leads to divisions and legalism within the body. It's as though their hearts grasp his salvation, but reject his redemption. The church confused these terms for too long.

Yes, salvation is a key part of the redemptive work, but to view the work of Christ as anything less than complete negates its power and working in our lives. This negated power causes questions toward the Holy Spirit's role in a believer's life.

You may ask how a seal equates to relationship. Jesus approached the world knowing death would be the result of His love. For the world to be free of the enemy's dominion, He had to redeem it. The work on the cross was redemption. When He rose three days later, the victory of Christ became our victory, and his Resurrection became our resurrection.

Earlier we saw the stipulations for redemption of mankind written on the scroll sealed in Heaven. The seals broken mean calamity and judgement on earth, but our bridegroom, in love, took judgement from all who called upon His name. The seals He bore set us free and brought us into relationship with Him. The seal upon His heart and hand are an outworking of a believer's ability to call upon Him in times of need.

What is the difference between asking Jesus into your heart and asking Him to seal it?

Read 2 Timothy 4:8

What does the Lord grant those who love Him?

Read 2 Timothy 3:5

How does one appear Godly without the Holy Spirit's power?

Read Ephesians 4:30

Who sealed believers? What were we sealed for?

Prayer: Lord Jesus, set a seal upon my heart. Let all I am be Yours alone. My ears hear Your voice, my eyes see Your body in unity, and my heart cries out for the souls of the lost. Send me in Jesus name, amen.

Application: In Corinthians Paul, writes at length about the importance of remembering the Lord's Supper. Read 1 Corinthians 11 and take communion in remembrance of Him.

Burning Love

Many waters cannot quench love, neither can floods drown it. If a man would offer all the goods of his house for love, he would be utterly scorned and despised.

The Song of Songs 8:7

To quench love, one would have to put it out by some means. The bridegroom is telling the bride that nothing can put out the fervor of her love for Him. There are many who seek Him for salvation, rest, and comfort, but few seek Him for sacrifice of self and denial of the flesh. If a believer truly understood the vapor that is this life, they would happily endure these trials for the prize found in the next.

This mindset of living for eternity is lost on many, but Jesus points out to this bride that she is focused on those eternal concerns. Do we chase after accolades of men when there is pain next door? Are we so free of concern for self that we offer our lives to Him daily? His praise of her abandonment to His call is a 'well done' before reaching the judgement seat.

In Leviticus 6, we see the first usage of this word 'quench'. It's the word used to describe the never-ceasing flame of the altar of sacrifice. Our sacrifice of love should never be quenched by the trials and tribulations of this world. Many will scorn or scoff at this total abandon, but the Lord sees the heart and desire of the bride to meet the need of their salvation and deliverance.

How would you describe an unquenchable love?

Read Romans 1:16

In what is Paul not ashamed?

Read Galatians 6:17

What did Paul bear as proof of his preaching the gospel?

Read 1 Thessalonians 2:2

In what conditions did Paul share the gospel?

Read 2 Timothy 1:8

What should we not be ashamed in?

Prayer: Lord, only through You can we understand the importance of eternity. Let my heart be moved toward those who don't know You. Give me words to share and a hunger to see salvation received in Jesus name, amen.

Application: We often walk through life without a clear understanding of eternity. Spend time in prayer today with the Father and ask Him for a revelation on the importance of living for eternity.

Come Alongside One Another

We have a little sister and she has no breasts. What shall we do for our sister on the day when she is spoken for in marriage?

The Song of Songs 8:8

Every church and body of believers have those in attendance who have no inclination or desire to nurture others. They see Christian life as a source of blessing and provision failing to recognize that the world needs their testimony of Christ and their fellow believers need to be lifted up. The bride asks the bridegroom here for wisdom as to how she should deal with this mindset in the body.

In the book of Revelation, the church at Laodicea receives a stern rebuke from Jesus for their apathy towards Christian life. Their faith has become self-serving rather than self-denying. Apathy in a believer's life says, 'I don't care about your eternity since I'm okay.' But if our hearts are truly new creations, we will desire that all come to know this great salvation.

Revelation 3:20 states Jesus is at the door knocking, wanting to be let in so He may fellowship with them, but in their indifference to the call of God on their lives, Christ is ignored. Many today suffer from this spirit of apathy. They believe they have all they need, but in reality, they are poor in spirit, blind to truth, and naked without righteousness.

It's in the best interests of the church body to help stir these believers to action. Paul tells us to stir one another up to good works and love (Hebrews 10:24). If we fail to heed the call of discipleship and stir other believers up to it, they will not hear the righteous judge say 'well done good and faithful servant'. Let us stir one another to good works and love and enjoy the joyous marriage supper with multitudes.

Is there an area of your life you've felt indifferent? How did it affect your life as a whole?

Read James 2:17-20

What does faith without works lack? Where does this power come from? Who is considered foolish?

Read Ephesians 4:3-6

How many bodies are there? Why must we all work together?

Read 1 Corinthians 16:13-14

What does Paul implore the Corinthian church to do?

Prayer: Lord, I pray today for a fresh stirring of the Holy Spirit in my heart and in the hearts of believers. Let us come together with a spirit of unity and harmony to share the gospel with all people. I ask for grace and even more grace to accomplish Your will and purpose in Jesus name, amen.

Activation: Ask the Lord how you can help stir other believers to discipleship.

Choices

If she is a wall [discreet and womanly], we will build upon her a turret [a dowry] of silver; but if she is a door [bold and flirtatious], we will enclose her with boards of cedar.

The Song of Songs 8:9

We are all given choices. Each and every day there are choices for life and blessing or death and cursing. The Lord responds to the bride's question about this sister who suffered from apathy. Does she fortify herself against the attacks of the enemy? Does she return to her first love? If so, a change will happen in her, and she will again be a wall for the Lord with battlements upon her.

The strong walls that fortify cities don't allow the enemy to come in and cause mayhem. The wall this sister builds is her defense against the thoughts, schemes, and devices of the enemy. She again begins nurturing the inner life where the king resides.

Not all will repent of their apathy. Some will continue to leave the door open to the enemy's influence and suffer under his reign. The open doors are as varied as sin. Some may feel unworthy of the King's affections and shy away from intimacy with Him. Others realize that a life wholly devoted to Christ means laying down their will for the Father's, and will refuse. What then should we do?

The bridegroom tells the bride to enclose them in boards of cedar. In Jude we read of the influx of false teachers into the body of Christ. It was Jude's desire that all would know and understand the imperative need to rid the body of those who preached a false doctrine which entered by 'the side door' (Jude 1:4).

They are the those who scoff at the cross of Christ and the need for repentance. Inside this particular body, James tells us they abuse the grace of Christ and refuse to live a life of holiness dedicated to Him. Later in the chapter, they are described in detail as those who don't understand the Word and deny the Holy Spirit.

Satan has ever ceased in his work to destroy the body of Christ, though his schemes change shape over time. One can see how these false teachers can sully the church and cause others to walk away from the Father. Sound doctrine and fortified faith in the Word are necessary, and it is the responsibility of mature believers to see that those who enter the body are not Satan's bait.

How might Satan try to divide a body of believers? Have you seen similar issues within the body?

Read Jude 1:18

What is a scoffer? How can a scoffer lead another astray?

Read Jude 1:22-23

Who should be refuted? Who should be treated with mercy?

Read Acts 20:28-30

What are mature believers called to do for the body? What happens when a church body lacks mature Christians?

Prayer: Thank You, Lord, that we are not subject to the enemy's schemes for division and strife. I pray that the enemy's attempts to deceive the body would be stopped, in Jesus name. I praise You that I hear the Holy Spirit who speaks when wrong teachings are given, so that I may guard my heart in Jesus name, amen.

Application: As a mature believer, it's imperative we measure everything by the written Word. There may be times when we hear teaching that is contradictory or incomplete. How should we address these instances? Spend time today asking the Lord for His view.

Secure in Him

[Well] I am a wall [with battlements], and my breasts are like the towers of it. Then was I in [the king's] eyes as one [to be respected and to be allowed] to find peace.

The Song of Songs 8:10

The bride exclaims to the king that she is set apart for His work and His direction. Her heart's desire is the same as the Lord's. When we approach our lives in service to the world, we are arrayed like this wall with its towers. The enemy doesn't have free reign in our minds and hearts to think or do evil against the unsaved or other believers.

This bride knows the difference between her righteousness and her holiness. When we make Jesus our Lord, we gain right standing with the Father, which is our righteousness. This right standing allows us to approach the Father without the veil in place, and His promise is that He hears us (John 9:31).

This right standing does not mean we are wholly devoted to His will and purpose, or that we do not fall into sin and condemnation. Holiness means to be set apart from, dedicated to something, or sanctified in our heart. For believers, our holiness is to be set apart and dedicated to the will and purpose of God. To know that holiness is possible and right standing is already ours, peace can reign in our heart and mind.

Explain the difference between holiness and righteousness.

Read 1 Peter 1:15-16

How does one live in Holiness? Who called us to be holy?

Read Romans 3:22

How does righteousness come?

Read James 3:18

Who gathers a harvest of righteousness? What is this harvest?

Prayer: Lord, I pray that You would cleanse my thoughts and my heart of all unholy things. Reveal to me any wrong motives or beliefs and anything that is displeasing to You, in Jesus name, amen.

Application: Spend time in prayer today asking the Lord about holiness. Is there anything He is asking of you? Write down what you hear in your journal.

The True Vine

Solomon had a vineyard at Baal-hamon; he let out the vineyard to keepers; everyone was to bring him a thousand pieces of silver for its fruit.

The Song of Songs 8:11

The opening statement of this verse is unique in its form. We know from our previous studies that Solomon, meaning peace, is a type of the prince of peace who is Jesus Christ. The vineyard He speaks of is that place where the bride has toiled sowing the truth of His redemptive work. This place is Baa-hamon, which means Lord of a multitude.

The body of Christ consists of multitudes who were brought into right standing with the Father through the consistent diligent effort of the bride. These keepers of the vineyard are to bring back one thousand pieces of silver for the fruits of it. An interesting correlation to a story we find in Genesis 20.

In this chapter, we have the incident involving Sarah and the King Abimelech in Gerar. This is following Abraham's great intersession for the cities of Sodom and Gomorrah. As Abraham and Sarah travel through unfamiliar lands, he instructs her to say she is his sister as he did previously when they traveled through Egypt and she was taken to the harem of Abimelech.

The Lord visits the king in a dream and warns him to not sin against Him. Though Abimelech was innocent, God intervened on Abraham's behalf. When the king returns Sarah, he chastises Abraham for his falsehoods, and we see this great man of faith making excuses for his actions.

The main source of Abraham's deception was fear. He lied and sacrificed his wife to save himself. The fear was based on a very common faulty premise that Christians fall into, and it is the belief that God will only use believers, and that the unsaved are immune to the influence of heaven. The more mature we become as believers the easier it is to see the sin of others and feel secure in superior morality.

The second excuse is really the most sinister and rampant in Christianity today. It is true that Sarah was Abraham's sister, but that fact was used in a way that conveyed falsehood. Abraham and many believers defend themselves with technicalities that are true yet they neglect being entirely truthful.

In the end, Abimelech responded by restoring the honor of Sarah with one thousand pieces of silver. In our human nature, we fail because of fear because it's easier to excuse our actions with technical truths rather than repent. Our place as God's chosen royal priests doesn't exempt us from the need to repent when we make mistakes or allow our flesh to rule us.

God's grace and mercy is always reaching out to us and others. Let us learn this truth when we feel we are decidedly set apart and holy before the Lord. Pride will work in the hearts of new and mature believers, so even in this place of maturity we must fully lean on our Savior and the Holy Spirit for wisdom and guidance.

Has the Lord exposed an area where you have needed to repent and change your ways? When was this and what did you do?

Read Acts 5:27-29

Who must believers obey concerning the preaching of Jesus? Why must we not fear?

Read Acts 10:9-28

What did the Lord command Peter to do? Why did he refuse? What was the reason for this lesson (v.28)?

Prayer: You, God, are Lord of all. You give grace in all things, even in our failures. I repent and pray for wisdom and revelation how to pursue holiness. I thank You for grace and even more grace to overcome my flesh, in Jesus name, amen.

Application: Though Abraham was righteous because of faith, he still lacked in the area of holiness. Has the Lord been speaking to you about areas in your life where holiness is lacking? Pray for the Holy Spirit's empowerment to change, and see Him move mightily on your behalf.

Lord of All

You, O Solomon, can have your thousand [pieces of silver], and those who tend the fruit of it two hundred; but my vineyard, which is mine [with all its radiant joy], is before me!

The Song of Songs 8:12

When the hearts of believers have no fear in repentance, we work diligently alongside others in the body without need of falsehood. The heart of this bride is that the Lord sees her repentant heart and desire to move forward with Him. Her vineyard, entrusted to her by the Lord, is before her and ready to be tended.

The law says the Lord of the vineyard should be paid for the fruits, but the law of love in her heart says she does this work for His glory. The believers she now mentors bring her joy because her heart is fully in line with the bridegroom's desire. She says that to hunger and thirst after righteousness is the greatest reward.

Read Matthew 6:20

What are the treasures of heaven we lay up? How do we have a treasury in heaven?

Read Matthew 16:37

What is the bride's promise in this verse?

Read 1 Corinthians 3:8

Doing the works of the kingdom in this life, we receive a reward. Where and when do we receive it?

Read Revelation 22:10

Summarize this verse in your own words.

Prayer: I thank You, Lord, that when I pray You hear me, and when I repent, You are quick to forgive. I pray for those I've lead to You. I ask for their hearts to be comforted by the Holy Spirit. I pray that every hindrance standing between them and Your will be removed, in Jesus' name, amen.

Application: Take time today to pray for those you've led to Christ. Ask the Lord if there is a person on your list who needs someone to stand in the gap in prayer. How will you pray for them today?

Shout for Joy

O you who dwell in the gardens, your companions have been listening to your voice—now cause me to hear it.

The Song of Songs 8:13

Those in the garden have heard the voice of the bride extoling the virtues of her bridegroom. They listen and are attentive to the voice of one who has matured in love and grace. Now the bridegroom tells her to focus on speaking to Him.

Maturity and growth will cause our influence to spread wide for the Lord. Many will come to hear wisdom and see the manifest fruit's intimacy with the King brings. We must always be mindful that our Lord desires our time and affections. It's a subtle reminder that He is always waiting to bring us closer to Him, and though we bring many into the kingdom, our first love has first place.

Do you find yourself too distracted by doing the work of the kingdom to seek Him?

Read Philippians 3:8

What is a priceless privilege? What did this privilege cost?

Read Colossians 2:1-3

Why did Paul struggle? Why did he want to see the church members so badly? What was his greatest hope for the members?

Read Psalm 42:1-2

What is David's heart desire? What is your greatest desire?

Prayer: Today, ask the Lord what you should pray for. Learning to lean on Him in all things is a practice worthy of pursuit.

Come, Lord Jesus

Make haste, my beloved, and come quickly, like a gazelle or a young hart [and take me to our waiting home] upon the mountains of spices!

The Song of Songs 8:14

Come Lord Jesus, come. It's the cry of all hearts turned toward the King. There will come a day when Jesus, the Righteous One, comes to gather His beloved bride and all the earth will declare the glory of the Lord. It will be a great yet terrible day. Great for those who have called upon His name and terrible for those whose hearts were hard and unrepentant.

The apostle Paul speaks of this desire in Philippians 1. He speaks of the desire to live this life for Christ, but he also speaks of the great promise all believers have in death to gain the presence of Him. We also have the great promise of the marriage feast where all will behold His greatness and the eternity to follow.

Come Lord Jesus, come and bring us into your heavenly habitation where we will be forever satisfied with Your presence and love.

Prayer: Psalm 46:1-5

About the Author

Sarah Neisen is a graduate of the New Day School of Ministry and Co-Founder of Discipleship Training Ministries. Along with her husband Lee, they seek to teach and encourage believers in their identity in Christ so that the Good News may be preached throughout the world with signs, wonders, and miracles.

She is a regular speaker at churches in the river valley region of Minnesota, and a guest speaker at women's groups and retreats. Sarah and her husband Lee have been married for 19 years and have one son whom she homeschools. They live on a farm in south central Minnesota.

Find out more by visiting her website at;

www.dtmssm.org

Don't forget to sign up for our newsletter. You'll get information on our ministry meetings, classes, and previews and discounts on all our upcoming books.

More By Sarah Neisen

30 Day Devotional Series Available on Kindle Unlimited

Days Filled With Grace: 30 Devotions for Mothers

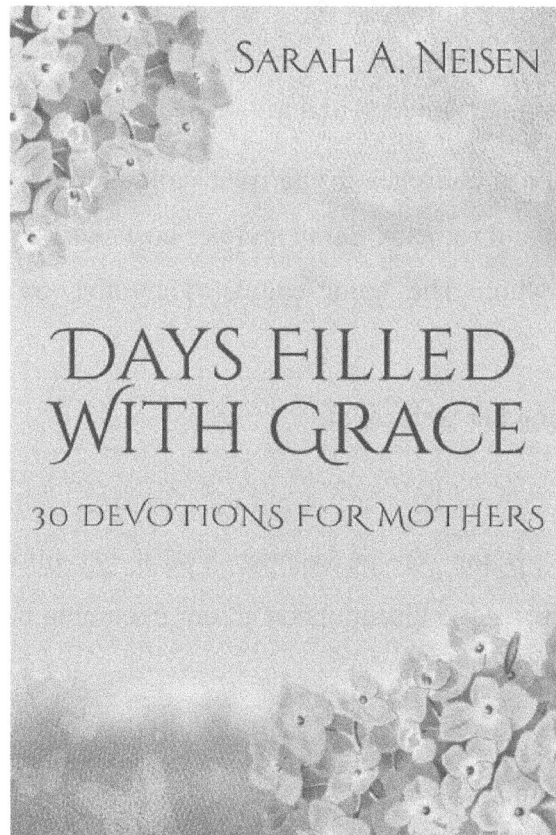

Coming Soon!

He Is True: 30 Devotions for Teens

You and Me: 30 Devotions for Singles